Travels in Shetland 1832-52

Travels in Shetland 1832-52

Edward Charlton

Edited by William Charlton

The Shetland Times Ltd.
Lerwick
2007

Travels in Shetland 1832-52

First published by The Shetland Times Ltd , 2007.

ISBN 978-1-904746-29-4

A CIP catalogue record for this book is available from the British Library.

Printed and published by
The Shetland Times Ltd.,
Gremista, Lerwick, Shetland,
ZE1 0PX, Scotland.

Travels in Shetland 1832-52

Contents

Biographical note

EDWARD Charlton was born on the 23rd of July, 1814, the second son of William John Charlton of Hesleyside in Northumberland. The memoirs of his sister-in-law Barbara Charlton, *Recollections of a Northumbrian Lady*,[1] give a vivid picture of the background. Of his mother, Mrs (Cholmeley) Charlton, Barbara says: 'Instead of the usual musical accomplishment, she acquired Latin, and she was also extremely well up in English literature. Her children grew up apace and soon gave Mrs Charlton plenty to do in teaching them the rudiments of knowledge, but so numerous were they[2] that a governess appeared early on the scene. Nevertheless, Mrs Charlton always helped in the teaching of her pet subjects, the grammar of dead and foreign languages, such as French, Italian and Latin.' The children also benefited from drawing lessons from Cotman, who taught for a time at Hesleyside, and other artists who visited the house in the summer to paint the Northumbrian landscape. Charlton used drawing on his travels as a modern traveller would use a camera.

At about the age of ten Charlton was sent to board at Ushaw College near Durham. Many years later Canon R. Frith wrote: 'I am only too glad to say that I was intimately acquainted with him in his earliest college days, being in the same class with him during his whole course. He was of a delicate, light frame of body, and was not distinguished as a prominent hero at the games of football and cat, but joined with spirit at the less boisterous games of racket and handball. He was greatly esteemed by all his schoolfellows for his great urbanity of manner and kindly disposition. He and I were always friendly and shared the same bedroom, which had formerly been used as the infirmary, facing the President's room. He always displayed a fondness for reading, and was an ardent student, and took good places at the *reading up*, though he had several strong competitors to contend with.'[3]

Charlton left Ushaw in October 1830, and the following year went to Edinburgh University to study medicine. Although on his own admission he was not at first an assiduous student, his account of his visit to Shetland in the summer of 1832 shows that he had acquired a good all-round knowledge of natural history. In the spring of 1833 his grandmother Mrs (Fenwick) Charlton died, and his parents shut up their house in Northumberland and went away for two years. Part of their absence from Northumberland was spent in Paris, and a visit he paid to France in 1835 (of which no journal survives) may have been mainly to see them. In the summers of 1833 and 1834, however, he stayed in the north. He made a second voyage to Shetland in 1834, and in 1833 he was in Western Sutherland, a district at that time hardly less remote. He mentions this in a later journal: 'In 1833 we had formed one of a large party which proceeded thither from Edinburgh chiefly for the purpose of botanising among its wild mountains and lakes, but there were several good anglers among our number, and Dr Greville, Jas. Wilson and Selby of Twizell[4] contributed not a little to supply our party of twenty one individuals with trout and salmon along our progress.'

He completed his doctorate at the age of 22 with a thesis on *The Lead Colic, as compared with the Colic of Poiton, West Indies.* That summer he went by sailing ship from Falkirk to Norway, then united with Sweden. He had the medical project of studying a form of leprosy that had vanished from other parts of Europe, but his journal deals mainly with social life in Christiania, the silver mines of Kongsberg, and long walks over extremely rough and often trackless country. He proceeded by sea from Brevik to Copenhagen, and was hospitably received into scientific and literary circles there. He returned by Kiel and Hamburg, having obtained a pretty good idea of medical practice in that northern part of Europe.

His journals for 1837-38 show him doing what is now called taking a year out. On the steamer from Hull to Rotterdam he ran into the explorer Charles Waterton and his journal gives an interesting glimpse of that famous eccentric. He travelled up the Rhine mostly by water and crossed the watershed to the Danube on foot. Nowadays we should think little of that. But mountaineering as a sport is generally reckoned to have begun only in the 1850s; the Alpine Club was founded in 1857; and Charlton's initiation into glissading over snowfields with an alpenstock took place twenty years earlier. He continued on foot to Salzburg, a distance of about 270 miles, before returning to vehicular transport, taking in the salt mines of Hallein en route.

He spent the winter of 1837-38 in Vienna, and on 26th January set off for Rome by diligence, passing through what is now Slovenia. Readers of *The Count of Monte Cristo* may remember how the Count spread his net for Albert de Morcerf at the Carnival in Rome, and how Morcerf joked sceptically about bandits. The dramatic date of this was 1838, and Charlton's journal not only describes the Carnival that year, but has a good deal to say about bandits both in central Italy and in Slovenia, then part of Austria, with the nearby frontier of Turkey offering bandits an easy refuge from the Austrian authorities. Immediately after the Carnival Charlton went down to Naples. There his passion for geology led him to spend a night on the top of Vesuvius. He returned to Rome for Easter, and his friends in the English community procured him the entrée to the Sistine Chapel for the Holy Week ceremonies and an audience with Pope Gregory XVI.

These journals close with Charlton's return to Hull in July, but according to a biographical notice by J. Embleton Smith[5] he now 'proceeded to Paris, where he entered the famous school of medicine in that capital', and 'produced a work – his first recorded technical exposition of the kind – on "Pneumonia as it Affects the Aged"', which was published in the *Collection des thèses* of 1839-45.

Back in Newcastle in 1839 Charlton started both to practice medicine and to lecture on medical jurisprudence at the new Medical School which had been founded in 1832. In 1841 he transferred to the lectureship on the Practice of Physic, and in due course he became Professor of Medicine, President of the College and, in 1870 when it met in Newcastle, President of the British Medical Association. This academic work did not prevent him from having an extensive general practice not only among the landowners and merchants but among the non-paying poor. In 1842 he married Eliza Kirsopp, the daughter of a Northumbrian Catholic family. The couple moved into 7 Eldon Square, a handsome house on the only side of the square that has survived recent developments in the centre of Newcastle. Charlton was now extremely busy, and did not have another holiday till he made his third trip to Shetland in 1852, though he found time to make substantial contributions to the *Dublin Review, Archaeologia Aeliana* and the *Tyneside Naturalists' Field Club Transactions*. He was a real polymath, and his publications on medicine are much exceeded in bulk by works of local history and archaeology, papers on ornithology and volcanology, and essays on the literature of Northern Europe. Besides the languages he was taught by his mother, he was acquainted with German, Danish, Norwegian and Icelandic.

After his return to Shetland in 1852, Charlton was able to take a short holiday nearly every summer, usually to Sutherland or Norway. In May 1862 Eliza died. Referring to this time, Barbara Charlton says in her *Recollections:* 'I was then accustomed to measure everybody by the yardstick of dear Eliza Charlton's perfection of character, a standard to which few mortals could attain.' She thought the widower did not mourn long enough. In fact it was two years before he remarried, and perhaps he did well not to delay further. His first marriage had been childless, and by the time of his second he was forty-nine, with only ten years left to live. His second wife was Margaret Bellasis, daughter of the Edward Bellasis to whom Newman dedicated *A Grammar of Assent*. When Charlton died, on 14th May, 1874, he left her five sons and one daughter, the youngest son still unborn.

A letter of 3rd April, 1914, from Sir George Otto Trevelyan of Wallington, referring to one of Charlton's historical writings, gives a glimpse of him in his later years: 'I well know Dr Charlton's excellent piece, of old days, and I knew him. I think that one of the reasons for my liking the Rev. Mr. Silvertop's company is that, in his black suit and homely distinction as of the 18th century, he reminds me of Dr Charlton.' The Silvertops were, in fact, related to Charlton through the Englefields, a family from which Charlton is said to have inherited the retentive memory that made him a man of such wide learning.

Charlton appears to have kept journals in shorthand of most of his travels. He then wrote them up in manuscript books, illustrated by his own drawings and watercolours, and sometimes had artists base more finished watercolours on his sketches. Unfortunately neither the shorthand notes nor the illustrations have survived for his visits to Shetland in 1832 and 1834; this is the more regrettable since there were once watercolours of Shetland scenes by George Richardson and T. M. Richardson. For these two visits we are dependent on typescript copies made by his son William Lancelot in 1909. For the 1852 visit we have a magnificent manuscript written by his wife Eliza with watercolour illustrations probably by himself.

The spelling of proper names varies. I have tried to modernise it and make it consistent, but I have preserved some spellings that are now out of date when it was clear that he was accustomed to them.

NOTES:

1   Ed. L.E.O. Charlton, London, Jonathan Cape, 1949
2   Nine, besides three that died in infancy.
3   Letter to Francis Kirsopp (Charlton's brother-in-law) dated 12th November, 1988. 'Cat' is a supposedly Anglo-Saxon game surviving only at Ushaw.
4   A Northumbrian neighbour.
5   *Newcastle Weekly Journal and Courant*, 3rd July, 1909.

Shetland 1832[1]

Voyage and Quarantine

ON the 7th July 1832 I embarked on board the schooner *Magnus Troil*. Our ship certainly could not boast either of imposing size or inviting cleanliness, but it was well manned for the coasting trade, having at least as many hands on board as the collier brigs between London and Newcastle. It being summer, the vessel was crammed with passengers. The main cabin, about twelve feet by eight, had to contain as constant residents not less than nine gentlemen, and at dinner, ladies and all, we mustered twenty-one. The accommodation was, to say the best of it, but indifferent; however, considering the low price of the passage (one guinea including provisions), we could not with justice complain. I had been unfortunately too late in applying for a berth, all were occupied, so that I gladly accepted the offer of my friend Mr Henderson of Gloup, to share with him his narrow couch. But when we got into the open sea, I did not find it advisable to rest so near a sea-sick passenger.

And here, as on shipboard there is ample leisure for taking of notes, I may as well note down the names and callings of my fellow passengers, for many, if not all, will be mentioned in the course of my narrative again. Imprimis was Mr Deans, a rich East India merchant of Shetland extraction, who had come out on a visit to his father, a retired shipbuilder of Lerwick. Captain Cameron, a gentleman of Unst, with his lady and three daughters, Miss Macrae and Mrs Henderson of Gloup with her two sons formed the elite of this crew.[2] Gavin Goudie, Hugh Jameson, Thomas Strong, William Hunter and William Johnson, all merchants of Lerwick; and lastly an old

The topsail schooner Magnus Troil *by P. Henderson.* © *Shetland Museum*

man of the name of Charles Scott, who was a singular example of extensive reading with very little previous education.

The clocks sounded eleven p.m. as we cleared the harbour of Leith, and even then many of our passengers were too late, and were forced, at the peril of their lives if we may judge from the looks they put on, to follow us for some distance in small boats ere they could rejoin the ship. It was late indeed ere I could close my eyes. All was strange and new to me. I was at sea for the first time in my life, my voyages had hitherto been confined to the Firth of Forth and only once or twice had I sailed down as far as the Isle of May to shoot sea fowl on its rocky coast. The noise overhead, the creaking of the masts, and above all the close, heavy air of the cabin which seemed as though produced on purpose to stifle the little remains of life within you, all so excited my attention that I never thought of sleeping.

At eight the next morning (it was Sunday) I was roused by a horrid grating noise overhead. I no longer wished to remain below, but earnestly desired to breathe again the fresh air and to see what way we had made during the night. But the deck at that time of day was no very comfortable station. Bibles were in great use, but it was not a book but a bath-brick that rejoiced in this strange appellation, and no doubt was so named from the crew being obliged, when using them for scrubbing the deck, to go down upon their knees. And where was now our good ship lying? Why, very nearly on the same spot where she was the night before: a few miles to the eastward of Inchkeith with the wind right ahead but light. The tide too was just now against us, but that we needed not to trouble ourselves about. The day was fine and mild, a great many vessels appeared in sight, and as we tacked in the narrow firth and approached the land on either side, the church bells sounded from the shore and mingled solemnly with the hoarse dash of the waves upon the rocks.

But though the wind was light and the sea comparatively smooth, many of the passengers began already to look pale and to avoid going below or even peeping down into those regions redolent of musty cheese and bilge water. The ladies did not appear upon deck, and my bedfellow proved a most wretched sailor, for he never moved from his berth or ventured to eat anything but a biscuit until we came in sight of the Shetland Isles. Such, however, did not prove to be the case with me. I was never better in my whole life.

By 10 p.m. we were fairly out of the Firth of Forth and were off the Bell Rock light, which flung its broad and varying beams far upon the waves. Soon after I retired to sleep, but not on my berth, for I could not persuade myself to sleep with such a personification of all that is wretched as my sea-sick companion. I therefore contrived to muster a number of great coats, cloaks and of the various coverings with which voyagers bedeck their upper man, and disposing some above and some below me, I was soon asleep on the end locker of the cabin.

On Monday morning, July 9th, I was awakened by the violent pitching of the vessel. I dressed and went on deck, but nothing was to be seen, save that it was a dead calm and the heavy mist lay so thick around that the nearest billow alone was visible as it rolled heavy and dark below the ship and caused sad cries of woe to ascend from the cabin. The ground swell, for such this was, to my unnautical eyes and feelings appeared tremendous, and not a breath of air was felt to steady the vessel. Still we rolled on all day, and a weary day it was, for of course none of the ladies showed themselves and very few of the gentlemen. At night we were off Aberdeen, and ere I retired to bed I could see the light of Buchan Ness, the extreme North-east point of Aberdeenshire, and the last land that we should see till our arrival in Shetland.

Tuesday July 10th At five this morning I was awakened by the steward, who said that a passenger in the forecastle was very ill and desired to see me as he understood I was a doctor. Really, thought I, I am commencing practice in good time. I had not studied medicine much more than a year, and that with no great assiduity.[3] Well, but they had dubbed me 'doctor', so go I must. I arose and proceeded to the forecastle, as dim and dark a hole as ever poor wretch was immured in on the wide waters. Here I found my patient, certainly very unwell, and apparently labouring under indigestion, for he had come on board in a state approaching starvation. The day before I saw him he had eaten so ravenously of boiled salt beef that the mate had positively refused to allow him any more. There was hardly any medicine on board, but what I had or could procure I administered to him, and then, climbing up the narrow hatchway, I stood upon the deck. It was a glorious morning. A fair wind had arisen during the night, and it now blew strong from the South-west.

About eleven p.m. the Captain climbed into the rigging and gave out from the crosstrees the joyful cry of 'Fair Isle on the weather bow!' But this night we could not distinguish it from the deck. Shortly after, I was standing on the forecastle watching the ship's bows as they plunged heavily into the huge masses of water. The sun had set, but a strong light still beamed in the North, as is always the case in these high latitudes in summer. Suddenly a small shadow as of a spirit of the deep flitted under the bowsprit, passed and repassed, and at times hovered with a fluttering, uneasy motion on the surface of the ocean, keeping generally two or three yards in advance of the ship. Hardly light enough remained for me to see distinctly the nature of the apparition, but I guessed it in a moment to be the terror of sailors, the wandering, persecuted Stormy Petrel. But to us it betokened no ill, and I hailed its appearance as a native of the isles I was about to visit.

Wednesday, July 7th. At six this morning all hands were on deck to look at the Fair Isle, which was now on the weather quarter and distant about eight miles. But before breakfast was announced, another and a far more important object occupied our attention. Sumburgh and Fitfield [Fitful] Heads, the scenes of *The Pirate*, rose in blue and rounded masses before us. Midday arrived, but with it came driving mist, and though the wind was fair from the SSW and the vessel made considerable way, we were denied a view within less than ten miles distant of these celebrated South headlands of Shetland. At two p.m. we were, according to the Captain, in the Roost of Sumburgh, but this day as on every subsequent occasion the Roost was smooth and tranquil, for we ran through it when the tide was turning, and this dreadful spot was consequently unruffled by the opposing currents.[1]

On a sudden, as I was leaning over the bows, two yawls full of, to me, strange looking mortals broke through the mist, pulled astern of the ship without hailing and disappeared in the driving fog. They were Shetland fishermen, the first I had ever seen, and I shall never forget the impression their strange garb made upon me. Dressed in their skin coats and breeches, with their nether limbs encased in huge boots, they rather resembled the pictures we have seen of some of the Esquimaux tribes, though having since had an opportunity of comparing these strange garments, I must confess those of Shetland to be decidedly inferior in point of manufacture. However the long fair hair of the Shetlanders, escaping in curls down upon their shoulders from beneath their large pendant caps of variegated worsted, certainly gave them a more picturesque appearance than the inhabitants of the more northern clime. Their boats, extremely sharp at both ends, with an extraordinary spring fore and aft, were not the least curiosity about them, and the rapid glance I caught of the whole as they burst suddenly through the fog, and were as quickly reinvested in its heavy canopy, imparted an air of romance exceedingly in accordance with my feelings of enterprise.

The wind now became adverse and we were forced frequently to tack, and by that means were often brought very close to the shore. So dense, however, was the fog that though we heard distinctly the hoarse murmur of the breakers on the rocks and the screams of the sea birds from their nests on the cliffs, not a glimpse could we obtain of the shore.

It was late in the evening when the mist dispersed and we found ourselves at the entrance of Bressay Sound, the best harbour in the British dominions, which perhaps has not its equal in the whole world. The sun was just setting and the ladies had come up from below to enjoy the delightful air on deck, and we discoursed of the quarantine we were to undergo. I remember well with what intense curiosity I gazed upon every bird and rock and house and field, and how I wondered that all on board were not equally astonished with myself. I have since visited several countries, but none, excepting perhaps Norway, have I entered with that feeling of awe, if I may so term it, which impressed me when entering the harbour of Bressay Sound on the 11th July, 1832.

As we swept slowly up the Sound we passed many small boats fishing for sillocks, the fry of the coalfish, which forms a good part of the food of the poorer classes in Lerwick. We hailed some of the boats but they fled from us as though our ship were the Flying Dutchman's grisly barque, or the famous schooner of Gow the pirate returned to terrify the inhabitants of these peaceful isles. I was surprised to see how many of the boats were rowed by women. At length we came off the town, but the night was too thick to enable us to distinguish with accuracy the different houses.

We knew that we were by law in quarantine, and that therefore we could not attempt to land, but a still more cogent reason kept us quiet in the shape of a King's cutter alongside, which would readily have taken upon itself the pleasure of firing a few round shot into our hull, in case of any infringement of the quarantine laws. On this account none of the ordinary bustle of a ship arriving in port was to be observed. A solemn silence reigned around, broken only by the dull plash of the quarantine boat as it approached us from the windward side. There is an old saying of consequence being increased as authority lessens, and it was admirably exemplified here. With a loud voice the quarantine officer called to us to keep off the ship's side, and that the Captain alone was to be permitted to speak. The latter regulation was good enough, but to forbid our occupying any part of our prison that we chose was too ridiculous. A white rag was suspended to a staff on the ship's stern; it was intended, no doubt, to be yellow, and truly time and weather had imparted to it something of that tinge. But paler far was the visage of the quarantine officer as he held up in one hand a lantern and in the other a long forked stick to receive our letters, for by a prodigious stretch of generosity we were allowed to send them on shore. Our guards represented the people on shore as being in the utmost terror of the cholera, and that even were the quarantine taken off by the authorities, the inhabitants of Lerwick would never permit us to land. This was heavy news indeed, but at that time we considered it exaggerated, so after a few hearty anathemas against the quarantine laws and the cholera as the cause of them we all retired to rest.

Thursday July 12th. How foreign is everything around me. Fields without hedges, a fort without soldiers, a town a sea port without wharves or piers, and a country all without a tree: how different, how wild and yet to my eyes how strangely beautiful. Our ship lay at anchor in a smooth and glassy sound, surrounded on all sides by land so that we could scarce discover the entrance through which we had passed in the previous evening. Bressay Sound is, as I have before mentioned, one of the finest harbours in Europe, being capable of containing the whole British Navy in perfect security. It has moreover the advantage of a double entrance or mouth, one to the South, the other to the North, so that ships may leave it at any time of tide or in any direction of the wind. Its depth varies from ten to fifteen fathoms, with a good bottom, and high lands lie chiefly to the North-west and East, consequently affording excellent protection to vessels from the two most violent winds that here prevail. Here, thought I, are we, prisoners without a crime, to rest for the space of six long days and nights, and each hour seems to me an age till I can set foot in the strange land I see before me. Still some of my fellow passengers cherished strong hopes of relief, and accordingly after breakfast a note was concocted and dispatched to the magistrates of Lerwick. Towards evening, for so dignified a body must have due time to digest both their dinners and their decrees, the answer was returned that no possible exception could be allowed in our favour.

This, as may be imagined, by no means increased our joy, but another cause of anxiety now began to show itself on board of our own vessel. On our arrival in port we had reported all hands as well on board, but in reality we had a sick man among us whose case, at that time unimportant, now began to excite our most serious attention. The individual alluded to was Alexander Robertson, the same man whom I had been called up to see two mornings before, but who had since so far recovered as to be able to sit upon deck. The confinement, however, on board of the ship along with his frequent errors of diet began to increase his disorder, and on the next day, Friday 13th, he was so ill that we resolved to apply for medical assistance from the shore. A letter was accordingly written by Captain Cameron requesting that Mr (alias Dr) Spence, one of the surgeons of Lerwick, might be allowed to come off to visit the sick man, but no answer was returned on that day, and poor Robertson continued to get worse. On the following morning, Saturday 14th, a note arrived from Dr Spence saying he did not consider the case of Robertson as requiring immediate attention. No statement, however, of the poor man's symptoms had been transmitted to him, and he must have been aware of this by a kind of intuitive inspiration. The whole ship's company were indignant, and well they might be, at such an answer, but few or none doubted that the real reason for his refusal was fear of the cholera.

Already had an idea begun to prevail in Lerwick that all was not right on board of the *Magnus Troil,* and on the arrival of our note requesting medical aid the pallid magistrates met in trembling consistory, while the anxious people crowded round the doors of the Town Hall to learn the result of their deliberations. Another note was soon dispatched from our ship to the effect that the case required immediate medical aid and stating that we would hold the magistrates responsible for any evil consequences that might ensue from so unwarrantable a delay. I drew up a concise account of our patient's symptoms, in as good and learned medical language as I was at that time master of, and concluded by saying that I could not and would not take upon myself any responsibility in the case. A copy of this document I still possess; it is really a curiosity of its kind and contains less of medicine than spleen and pretty broad language against the magistrates of Lerwick.

The representation had its desired effect, and between five and six p.m. a boat was seen slowly pulling towards our vessel, and on coming alongside we discovered in it Doctors Barclay and Cowie, though to say the truth, the one was but a surgeon and the other had no medical honours whatsoever. As they came within hail they said they had been sent by the magistrates to examine the sick man, but at the same time were strictly prohibited from touching either him or anything else on board. They called me to them and I for some time refused to go, as in doing so I should in some measure involve myself in their transactions. At length at their earnest request I went down with them into the fore cabin and there Dr Cowie and I examined the patient. The great Barclay, a little round, dull, heavy, paunchy creature, descended the ladder, looked for a few minutes at the countenance of poor Robertson and then turned to the hatchway and scrambled up on deck with the most wondrous agility. On leaving the vessel they told me to give him some medicine, which was certainly rather a superfluous recommendation as there was none on board of the vessel. It was evident also that they were very anxious to shift the responsibility from their own shoulders onto mine, and this made me rather uncivil to my professional bretheren on this occasion. It was also evident to me that the poor man was fast sinking. A gloom had already spread over the ship's company, the sailors congregated in groups on the ship's forecastle, but one or two ventured below, and the dying man, for such I now considered him, was watched only by his wife and a single old seafaring man. Early next morning, Sunday, we received a visit from Mr Barclay. As he came on board he asked me if I had seen the sick man since he left. I said 'No! For it is your report and not mine that will be received by the magistrates.' He said nothing but walked forward. I was told that he looked at the man and then retired hastily from the bows. Such, said he, was the excited state of the town that the people would hardly permit the doctors to land on their return from the plague-stricken ship.

As soon as Dr Barclay had gone I hastened down to see the poor patient, whom I found in a dying state. He was the first person I had ever seen die, the first in whom I had ever seen life receding step by step before its overpowering adversary, Death, and though I have since faced the grim tyrant in many more horrid shapes, none affected me more than this. True, time has hardened me in this respect, but I was on this first occasion in a strange land, surrounded by new faces, and altogether in a situation totally different from my usual habits. The poor wife of Robertson was a really handsome young woman and had been born to a better station in life than that which she now occupied. They had four children, the eldest not more than six years of age, and the poor little things played quite unconsciously about the cabin, or ventured occasionally up onto the quarterdeck to receive a kind word or a biscuit from some of the richer passengers. The second boy was a particularly handsome child, and this gave them an additional interest among the kind hearted young ladies on board, and we all knew they had nothing to depend upon save the exertions of their father who was now, alas, past all hope of recovery.

Monday, July 16th, closed the sufferings of poor Alexander Robertson. I was at his bedside till a late hour on the previous night, and early in the morning was again at my post. The crew, I observed, had almost all slept on deck, for the fear of a dying man and the still more potent dread of the cholera had driven them entirely from the cabin where the sick man lay.

Early in the morning we received another visit in form from all the three doctors of Lerwick, one of whom ventured no further than the gangway, the second looked down the forehatch upon the face of the dying man, and but one, Mr Cowie, descended to his bedside. The result was that they pronounced the patient to be in immediate danger of death, an opinion long entertained by everyone on board. Having promulgated this sage conclusion, and having made us pass in review before them that they might spy the lurking cholera in our countenances, they retired in all haste, one of the three observing as he went over the vessel's side that he felt quite sick already. Prepossessed in this way it was not wonderful that they should proclaim the case to be 'a very suspicious one of cholera' – I give the opinion verbatim.

I sate by the bedside of poor Robertson nearly the whole day. I knew all was in vain, but still I thought it might console his wife to see 'the doctor' so near. At half past four he had fallen into a complete stupor with hard and stertorous breathing; in fact the soul had no longer power over the prostrate body. Six o'clock came and I thought it was his last hour. I was right. At half past six the death rattle suddenly stopped, poor Robertson was freed from his earthly cares. His wife and the single sailor before mentioned were all that assisted at this closing scene. When he had expired his poor widow sat silently down by the bed. The old sailor closed the eyes of the corpse and merely said 'He's gone', and at the sound of his voice the poor woman burst into tears.

I left the fore cabin and went aft to report his death. It created little or no surprise, all were aware of what was to happen, though I suspect some delicate souls had strong objections to passing the night with a corpse on board. The old sailor in the meantime laid out the body as decently as our circumstances would permit.

Great was the commotion among the good people of Lerwick when they learned that the poor man had actually expired. The great council of the magistrates met in the Town Hall, and the result of their sapient deliberations was soon communicated to us. By order of the magistrates we were placed under martial law, under the guns of His Majesty's cutter we were commanded to hoist the yellow flag at the mast head, as having cholera on board, and we were condemned to ride in quarantine for at least ten days more. Should any sickness occur on board during the additional probation, the terrible imprisonment would be extended to even a longer period. And really looking at the crowded state of the vessel I thought it would be sufficiently wonderful if we all remained in good health until the end of the week. However all this was not more than we had expected. We had not hoped for mercy from the law, and still less from its officers, and the King's cutter close alongside effectually prevented us from infringing any of the regulations.

But this was not all. The doctors refused to come on board to see the body, nor would the magistrates allow the only man of talent proficient in anatomy, Dr Arthur Edmonston, to come aboard to perform a post mortem. Dr Edmonston's errand under the conditions would not have been agreeable, but at the same time we would willingly have put up with it to be released from the totally unnecessary quarantine. Such was the growth of rumour on shore that it was reported and believed that afternoon in the town of Lerwick that two of the poor man's children had already fallen victims to the cholera. Poor little ones! They were in the best of good health, and were at this time probably the happiest beings on the ship. In addition to all these miseries we were now coolly told that we should not be permitted to send letters on shore even if fumigated. This last ordinance was a fatal one to the wise magistracy, for herein they far outstepped their authority. Late at night an order came from the shore that we were instantly to hoist the yellow flag, and must on the morrow commit the corpse of poor Robertson to the deep. We prepared tonight to comply with this injunction. The remains of the dead man were sewed up in a hammock, some heavy stones (for we had no 12 lb shot on board) were tied to his feet, and the body was laid out on some planks in the jolly boat at the stern. Had it not been for the cheerful good sense of one of our passengers, Mr Deans, whose real goodness of heart began daily to show itself more and more, we should scarcely have passed the night without some recriminations of no gentle kind.

And what a day of storm it was on the morrow. The wind whistled through the shrouds, the sea, even in the quiet harbour, rolled and roared as if impatient to burst the bounds of the land, and as the sun went down the gale increased and blew with tenfold fury. This conflict of the elements was in many ways particularly distressing to my fellow passengers. Many were owners of boats to a large amount in various fishing stations among the islands, and now that the main cause of our excitement had lost its power, and we knew the worst that could befall us in our watery prison, our attention was directed to the probable fate of others, and our fears for the safety of the boats increased with the violence of the storm. Sunday night had been tranquil and cloudless, all on board had rejoiced in the anticipation of a good fishing day on the morrow, and the sun rose on the Monday in all its splendour over a sea unruffled by a breath of wind.

Tuesday 17th July. I was on deck at an early hour, for the hideous howling of the coming storm effectually hindered any prolonged repose. We could scarcely keep our feet for the violence of the wind, even when partly sheltered by the bulwarks, and the Captain felt no small anxiety lest the ship should part her cable. By the confusion observable among the ships around us we could plainly see that the same fears were entertained by others.

In accordance with the orders received last night we hoisted this morning the quarantine flag. It was a bit of yellow silk which had been discovered somewhere on board. So frail a material was ill calculated to stand against a storm, in a moment, almost, it was blown to ribbons, and we were forced, pirate-like, to hoist a huge piece of black canvas to the mast head, black being, to the sailor's idea, the most unlucky colour next to the detested yellow. After breakfast we buried poor Robertson. The funeral ceremony was short indeed and sadly wanting in solemnity. The jolly boat was slowly lowered into the water, the mate descending into it raised the planks on which the corpse reposed, the body turned slowly over the gunwhale, and with a heavy surge and plash sank beneath the waves for ever.

NOTES:

1   This text is dated April 14th 1843; Charlton evidently edited his journal then, perhaps with an eye to circulating or publishing it.

2   William Cameron was married to Margaret Mouat and later took her name. Charlton describes him elsewhere as 'by far the best informed man that I met with in Shetland, though there was an air of the petit maître about him which essentially ruined him in the eyes of all his friends.'

3   The author might have added that he was only seventeen years old.

4   'The currents of the Atlantic and German oceans meet at this point.' (p.93 below)

Shetland 1832

The storm of 1832

I LITTLE thought at the time that the day would be one ever remembered in Shetland, and that 'da grit gale', as it has always since been termed, was then dealing such destruction among the poor Shetland fishermen. The details of this catastrophe are written partly from my own observations and partly from the many accounts I received from the relatives and companions of the sufferers.

On the day of Robertson's burial the storm was at its height. On the night he died the wind howled through the rigging and the lamp which, as an infested vessel, we were obliged to hoist at the foremast head was frequently extinguished. In the almost always smooth and glassy harbour the rolling of our ship was so heavy as to confine the ladies to their berths, but at that time we scarcely thought that any boats would be out on the open sea. Our minds were also occupied with the death of our fellow passenger and by the consequent extension of the term of our captivity, and it was not until the Tuesday that the roar and tumult of the elements attracted our particular attention.

It was indeed a fearful storm. The rain and sleet drove sharp in our faces as we paced the deck, and the white spray flew over our bows as plentifully as if we had been in the middle of the Atlantic. Certainly I at the time enjoyed thoroughly the tumult and roar of wind and sea, and as I saw no immediate danger likely to result to the inhabitants of the islands from the hurricane, the wild war of the elements, the screams of the sea fowl and the white foam of the seething billows relieved against the dark heather hills to the North was, to my imagination at least, a most soul-stirring scene. Suddenly a boat was seen approaching the cutter, the *Swan*, then close alongside of us. For a moment it was visible topping the foaming waves, and then disappeared on the other side of the cutter. A passenger on board of our vessel expressed a fear that some boats had been out, and might be missing. His surmise proved to be but too true. Immediately after communicating with the boat the cutter slipped her cable and, carrying all the sail she dared, swept out of the South entrance of the harbour.

All was now anxiety on board of the *Magnus Troil*. From the quarantine officers we shortly learned that some sixty boats, each manned by six hands, were that morning missing from the eastern shores of Shetland. They could give no account as to whom the boats belonged, but the cutter had gone out to save them if she could fall in with any still afloat in such a sea. This was but a faint chance indeed, for the gale hourly increased, and though the sky was clear, showers of sleet drove in our faces as we stood upon the deck. By means of a telescope we could see the whole town was in commotion. Groups of people were assembled on every small landing place anxiously awaiting the return of the cutter, or the arrival of some of the boats from the North.

The sails of a Dutch herring buss appeared above the point of land which shut out from our view the southern entrance of the harbour. On she came, dashing the spray from her heavy bows, and rolling with the waves like her prototype the porpoise. Every eye on the *Magnus Troil* was strained to see what was on her decks, but on her next tack she passed far to windward and anchored in safety amid the other vessels of her nation. We saw a boat leave her for the shore, and observed the people crowding round it as it touched the pier; but it was not till an hour afterwards that we learned she had brought in two boats' crews, though the boats themselves could not be saved from destruction.

In our imprisoned state it was but seldom we could get intelligence from the shore, and after for long pacing the deck I descended cold and weary to breakfast in the cabin, where but very few of the ladies were present. For a considerable time I remained below, but was roused by a sudden cry from the deck that a Dutchman was upon us. I rushed up the hatchway just in time to see the heavy, lumbering galliot barely clear our quarter, but so close was she that one could have tossed a biscuit on board. Our men eagerly hailed her as she passed for news of the boats. 'Six boats' crews on board and many boats seen bottom upwards' was the answer. She brought to at no great distance from us and our men attempted to keep up a conversation with the Dutch sailors through the howling storm, but could elicit no further satisfactory information.

After dinner we were again called up on deck, for the same vessel had parted her cable and was driving upon the Island of Bressay. However by great exertion she was at length brought up a few hundred yards to the leeward of our brig. Our own situation was at the time by no means an enviable one. Had we been driven on shore by the snapping of our cable we should have been exposed to the double dangers of shipwreck and of receiving very rough usage at the hands of the terrified inhabitants, so much did the fear of the cholera overpower all other considerations. During the evening a few more Dutch herring busses came in with some boats' crews on board, and throughout the whole night the lights in the houses in Lerwick remained unextinguished, and the inhabitants appeared to be all anxiously expecting further accounts of the terrible disaster.

Wednesday, July 18th, dawned and the storm was unabated. But little rain fell during the whole of the gale, but the salt spray driven up with great force by the gale prevented us from walking the deck with comfort. One of the first objects that met my eye on issuing from the cabin was a six-oared boat driving gallantly in through the North entrance of the harbour. She had saved the crew of another boat that had been swamped alongside of her, and so she consequently contained twelve men instead of six, which is the usual number of the crew of a fishing boat. It was a really beautiful but withal anxious sight to watch these poor fellows, of whom eight were lying at the bottom of the boat, one managed the helm, and the other three attended to the sail, as the boat dashed on through the heavy surf. As each white squall swept down, dashing up the spray in sheets into the air, we saw the sail lowered and then cautiously raised again, as the reed bends to the storm and rises again after it has gone by. The boat eventually arrived safely at the town, and the charitable assistance rendered by the original boat's crew to their distressed bretheren did not pass unrewarded.

About half past one the cutter was seen coming back into the harbour, and brought up in her old position between our vessel and the shore. The unfortunate herring buss before mentioned had nearly suffered another disaster, for in bringing up the cutter they fell foul of the Dutchman, but the cutter was the only sufferer in snapping her yard across the middle so that it hung down in two pieces. They had saved but one boat's crew, and though I cannot state it as a fact, I was told afterwards that the commander of the cutter had been misled or misinformed as to the exact situation of the boats, and indeed he had quite enough to do to take care of his own vessel when he got outside.

Such is all I know from personal observation of this terrible misfortune, by which the crews of eighteen boats, amounting to over one hundred men, and the very flower of the Shetland fishermen, met with a watery grave.

In travelling through the islands after my release from quarantine I heard many strange and wild stories and superstitions relating to this calamity. The wind from two or three days previous had been blowing steadily from the South-east, but the practised boatmen on the western coast of Yell, and indeed on the whole western side of Shetland, had observed an extraordinary swell setting in from the Atlantic, while on the eastern coast the water was comparatively smooth. I was also assured that for a day or two beforehand the North Yell fishermen had heard hollow moaning sounds proceeding from the deep, but these may be accounted for either by the swell breaking upon the rocks, or more probably by the exaggerating superstition of the inhabitants. Yet certain it is that during the solemn calm of nature that is so often the forerunner of a storm the swell upon the rocks assumes a louder and a deeper tone, and being audible to a much greater distance would require but a little stretch of the Shetlander's imagination to convert it into the foreboding signals of the spirits of the deep. But perhaps the most remarkable phenomenon of the storm was that the piltocks[1] or young of the *Gadus carbonarius*, which are generally used as bait for the deep sea fishing, were found in abundance and took freely on the East coast, while on the West there were comparatively none; at least few or none could be seen about the baits. Perhaps the seeing of the fish about the baits may appear extraordinary to some, but in the pure waters of these northern latitudes, anyone, and particularly the practised piltock fisherman, can discern at an immense depth beneath the surface any object moving around the bait. It is therefore believed by the Shetlanders a special interposition of

Providence that the men of the West coast should have been prevented by the want of bait from going out on that day which proved so fatal to their brother fisherman; but according to the accounts of many naturalists fish are well known to change their situation on the approach of a storm, though I cannot exactly coincide with the firm belief of the fishermen that they crowded under the East coast to shelter themselves from the coming tempest.

I was solemnly assured by an old, white haired fisherman of Fetlar that he and his companions saw a white boat with six men in white leather dresses, the same except in colour as they themselves wore and with similar white worsted caps upon their heads, running broadside to the stormy sea, and upsetting two boats alongside. The reader may judge of this for himself; the story of the Flying Dutchman at the Cape and its very simple explanation will probably occur to his mind. Why should not such phenomena exist in the Shetland seas? Captain Scoresby has seen ships in Greenland where no ships could be, and has even been able to make out by means of the refraction his father's vessel when she was yet several leagues below the horizon.

Three of the men belonging to this old veteran's boat were washed out of it by a heavy sea, but the returning wave to their utter amazement and great joy washed them back into the boat. 'Ah, Sir,' said the poor fellow to me in a tone that indicated his acute remembrance of that dreadful day, 'da sea wis so hie dat she hidit da Sun. We cud do noting else dan to back her into da Norroway cuist, and alwise seeking to keep her head into da wind and da watter, and dat did we not alwise.' And indeed I am told that some boats on sounding found themselves on the edge of the Norway bank in 20 fathoms of water.

An old skipper and his crew of young lads who did not reach Fair Isle until the Saturday sailed on one tack for thirty-six hours with a strong breeze before they came in sight of that island. A few more hours and their strength would have been exhausted; as it was, they had to be assisted out of their boat by the inhabitants of Fair Isle when they got in. These poor fellows had taken with them no other provision than their customary scanty stock of meal and water for three days, and this they had consumed upon the Thursday morning, having been out from the Monday previous in the open sea. Had a calm succeeded the gale, the fate of all would have been sealed, as they could never have possessed sufficient strength to row to the shore. Towards the end of the storm a boat containing several bodies was washed ashore on the beach near Sunae on the eastern mainland. The poor crew had probably pulled up close to the land when, their strength being exhausted, they had resigned themselves to their fate. Three or four miles further and their lives would have been saved, but they had no doubt already rowed ten times that distance against a headwind and a heavy sea.

In my excursions through Unst, Fetlar and the mainland it was indeed often a melancholy task to enter a cottage. There sat the poor widow silent and sad, and her speechless grief contrasted strongly with the poor little children playing round the fire all unconscious of their heavy loss. Sometimes two or three of these widows would be met together to bewail their common bereavement, and again and again did a mother, a wife or a daughter hurry out to me as I passed to ask for news of the boats. If perchance I had heard a report of any more having been saved their grateful eyes would glisten with hope, and the simple, pious exclamation of 'Oh God, dat der may be mongst dem my guidman' burst from their lips. Few cottages were there that had not to deplore the loss of a father, a brother or a son. In general the male part of the inhabitants bore their loss with silent resignation, but often in spite of all their firmness a tear would steal down their cheeks as they recounted to me the closing scene of a brother's or a father's life, when they saw him at one moment pulling as stoutly and as strongly as they could do, and the next he was swept away from their side. But the grand anchor of the widows' hope was the account brought by the *Norna* of an American outward-bound vessel which had hailed them when running before the wind to the effect that she had five boats' crews on board. This was indeed a strong ray of hope for the desolate. They told me they were sure of their husbands and friends being amongst the number, but alas, the joy of hope realised was reserved but for a few. It was in the month of January, 1833, that five of the lost men returned to their native islands having been actually carried out to America by the vessel which had hailed the *Norna*. But their skipper, the pride of the East Coast fishermen, was not of their number. He had been the last to leave the boat, and as he ascended the rescuing vessel's side a tremendous sea threw his own frail craft high into the air, and it descended with resistless force upon the head of the unfortunate man when thus on the very threshold of safety.

Such are the particulars of this disastrous storm, at the mention of which during the next hundred years the Shetlander will tremble and pray that such a calamity may never occur in his days.

NOTE:

1   Perhaps a variant for 'sillocks'. See the entry for Friday June 20th 1834.

Shetland 1832

Visit to Yell

OUR quarantine wore on wearily enough, the same routine system was pursued daily, and to this hour it seems as though I could accurately lay down the exact position of every bolt and trenail in the deck of the *Magnus Troil*. By a great stretch of magisterial condescension we managed to obtain a few novels from the shore, and by means of these and some petty quarrels among ourselves time was in some sort or other whiled away. I had with me a work on botany from which I amused myself by making drawings. This too served in some measure to lighten the tedium of quarantine until -

Thursday July 26th. All on board were in high spirits at the prospect of leaving the ship. At an early hour the whole company were mustered on the deck, looking out for the shore boat which would convey official intelligence of our release. At half past eleven a.m. the collector Fea came off and announced that the period of our detention had expired. Several boats which during the morning had been hovering about the ship now came alongside and in a short time were pulling with a full cargo of passengers for the shore.

As soon as I landed I called on Mr Ogilvy where, as I discover recorded in my Journal, I found good wine and indifferent children. Thence in company with Mrs Henderson's eldest son John, who was subsequently my constant companion through the islands, I walked along the shore to the south east of the town and gathered some Chitons amongst the stones within high water mark. They were almost all of the species *laevigatus*, but one Chiton Ruber rewarded me for my toil. The terminus of our walk was a lake on the right of the road to Scalloway. It was I believe on the banks of this lake that Dr Fleming shot a specimen of the Red-necked Phalarope, for this bird, though it breeds in Orkney, is yet extremely rare in Shetland, nor is it mentioned by Graba as occurring in Faroe. On an island near the centre of the lake as an additional object of interest to me were the foundations of an ancient 'Burgh' ['Broch'] or stronghold of the oldtime Norsemen.

Around the banks of this lake I found a large quantity of the Jasione Montana which is also mentioned by Neill, but in fact this plant abounds in every part of the Shetland Islands. Where ever there was any extent of soft turf it was covered with the plant whose lovely blue, contrasted with the equally abundant pink flowers of the Dianthus Deltoides, formed an agreeable carpet to conceal the rugged conglomerate rocks.

We returned to dine at the house of Mr Hay who is reputed to be by far the richest merchant in Shetland.[1] Riches no doubt are necessary to him for he has a family of thirteen or fourteen children. Strawberries are not unfrequently cultivated with success around Lerwick and we had a large dish of them this day from Mr Hay's garden.

We[2] had seen enough of Lerwick from the ship and were therefore exceedingly anxious to get away at once for the North Isles. No boat, however, was to be got till the following morning, at which time we engaged a boat to be ready at five a.m. to convey us to Yell. About 6 p.m. we crossed the sound to Gardie. I was much pleased with the excellent order in which Mr Mouat's grounds were kept, and the house too would not have disgraced a gentleman's park in England. In the drawing room a stuffed specimen of the Wryneck attracted my attention and I was informed that this poor wanderer from the south had been taken in Delting a few years before. I returned to supper at Mr Hay's and then proceeded to Lerwick to sleep at Mr Ogilvy's.

Friday July 27th. At five a.m. we got our luggage from the *Magnus Troil* and sailed for Cullivoe in Yell. We soon passed out of the North entrance of the harbour and cleared the conglomerate rocks of Rovie Head. Here I saw for the first time a great number of Shags and Black Guillemots around me, which tempted me beyond all measure to thin their flocks with my gun. Greenholm, a low but prettily perforated rock next attracted my attention, and to me it appeared an object of great interest as I was as yet unacquainted with the wonders of the Shetland coast. Before arriving at Whalsey we could make out the Skerries in the extreme distance on our right. These islands I never visited, for they presented nothing inviting to the naturalist, except that occasionally during the fishing season some remarkable corals, fish and shells are brought to shore by the boatmen. Close to Whalsey we passed the Noup of Nesting which, jutting out boldly into the sound of Whalsey, for a long time concealed from our view the lands that lay further to the north.

A light wind now carried us past the mainland, and after running through the Sound of Whalsey, the whole of the North Islands opened at once before us. The bold coast of Yell was near at hand, and the distant view was closed by the high hill of Sanafiord in Unst and by the Vord or Watchtower hill in Fetlar. We landed upon Lunna Holm in order to avoid the tremendous tides which run through Yell Sound. The Holm was soft and yielded agreeably to our feet which had so long paced up and down the hard decks of our prison ship. The island consists entirely of gneiss and is inhabited only by a few of the common gulls. Of course some sheep too were here, for the possession of a holm is in these parts as in Iceland a valuable and desirable property. The tide slackened after an hour or two and we sailed with a light breeze towards the coast of Yell. On a low rock I saw for the first time in my life a cluster of about twenty of the common green Shag Carbo Christatus. We still had the tide in our favour as we ran past the low, rich green island of Hascosea on whose eastern extremity may be observed one of the best examples of the basin shaped formation in the world. As we rounded the point of Burraness the tide we found against us, and the light wind we had up to this in our favour died entirely away. There was nothing for it but to pull for Cullivoe as hard as we could. We edged away close under the shore to avoid as much as possible the tide that boiled along from Blomel [Bluemill] Sound at the distance of half a mile from the land. When so heavy a current exists in the midstream, so to speak, there is always a sort of ebb or backwater to be met with close in shore on either side of the strait. But even with this advantage our labour was immense, and we all took a turn at the oars. I well remember taking the bearings of the different points when we commenced our heavy task, and how my heart sank within me when after an hour's exertion I discovered that he had advanced but a few hundred yards from the spot where I had first made my observation.

It was a lovely evening, and all was still and quiet save a few Black Guillemots which bobbed up and down on the edge of the boiling tide to pick up the numerous edible substances carried along by the stream. But we had no thought of disturbing them, all our efforts were directed to gain the pebbly beach of Cullivoe which we now saw before us. A wild cackling cry of a bird attracted my attention, it was a harsher scream than any that had hitherto fallen on my ear. Mr Henderson pointed towards the head of the voe, across which two Rain Geese or Red-throated Divers were passing to some lake in the interior of Yell. In passing the north point of Hascosea I had for the first time in my life met with the Shearwater Petrel, and then procured the only specimen of that bird that I brought home from this my first excursion.

At six p.m. we landed on the beach of Cullivoe and deposited our luggage in the buith or store house kept by Mr Pole. From thence we started for the mansion of Gloup carrying with us nothing but our guns and ammunition. Henderson expected me to prove but an indifferent bogtrotter but he had forgotten my apprenticeship upon the wild moors of Northumberland. Like the good Methodist minister on the road to Scalloway I did not walk, nor run, nor drive, but just 'loupit awa' over moss and moor and holt and hill till we came in sight of the mansion of Gloup, a goodly building of solid stone and fully exposed to every wind of heaven. But its walls would stand against a hurricane; two yards and a half of stone and lime would smile at a battery of cannon and in this country form no bad substitute for a grove of sheltering trees. All the inhabitants of the neighbouring cottages came out to greet us and joyously welcomed home Mr Henderson to his paternal property, nor did they forget to bid good cheer to 'da strainger lamm' who had come so far to visit their rocks and wilds.

Saturday July 28th. About ten a.m. we sallied forth with our guns in pursuit of game. I was soon attracted to the fishing stations near to which I observed many of the parasitic gulls whose black plumage and hawk-like flight contrasted strongly with the silvery hue of the Terns, Kittiwakes and Herring Gulls whom they ceaselessly persecuted. During my stay at Gloup I was generally pretty well accoutred for my various pursuits.[3] On one shoulder I carried a double barrelled gun and ammunition, the other shoulder was frequently balanced by my heavy German rifle, while on the one side hung my game bag and on the other a huge tin case into which I stowed away shells, plants and seaweeds, and in various pockets might have been found various smaller boxes, as safe receptacles for insects or for the finer shells. As I was on an island composed almost entirely of gneiss, I seldom took out my hammer except when on an excursion. I had discovered some fine garnets or Felspar crystals, for these were almost the only minerals afforded by the rocks of the island of Yell.

We walked along the shore to the north of Gloup house till it trended away to the east and then followed its windings as far as Houland. In the deep gios, some of which are quite inaccessible from the shore, we saw numbers of particoloured rabbits, the prevailing hue, however, was piebald of a light fawn and white colour. They were very wild and quick in their movements, so that I was quite unable to shoot any of them for dinner. They came, I was told, originally from a tame stock, that was turned out many years ago near Gloup, but on other islands the common grey rabbit is abundant and quite as indigenous as in England. Starlings in large flocks and singly were to be seen along the coast. They breed here in the crevices of the rocks and on my second visit to Shetland I discovered a nest of these birds thus placed on a cliff of the island of Vaila. In Shetland they are far more domestic in their habits than in more southern climes. I remember seeing at Colafiord in Northmavine that a number of starlings had made their nests under the hospitable eaves of a house in holes purposely left there by the rude architects of the building. Perhaps the pure northern air made me less particular in my food but I found the starlings when roasted so palatable that they frequently graced my supper table on subsequent occasions.

Beyond Houland the coast towards Papal Ness is indented by several deep bays, and occasionally the shore is bounded by high sand dunes resembling those upon the coast of Holland. Here too the sand has worked irreparable mischief. Many fine fields have been completely overwhelmed by this irresistible agent and in the south of Shetland a whole estate has been buried and lost for ever to the owner. We walked round the high banks beyond the dunes and entered the ruins of an old Catholic chapel, which now stood lonely and deserted on the banks of the little lake. Some of the rafters and beams of the roof yet remained, the walls were perfect, with the exception of the doorway on the west which was in ruins. The whole area of the building would not have held more than 60 persons. On looking about the eastern end, where no doubt the altar would have stood, I found a halfpenny of George III and on expressing my astonishment at this circumstance to Henderson, he assured me it was no doubt an offering from some of the fishermen, and stated that he had once found a silver coin of much more ancient date in a recess which he pointed out high in the wall. We waited for some time at the old chapel searching for coins among the ruins, until the rabbits which were abundant on the banks should again have ventured from their burrows. But such sport is not without its dangers. The burrows are often situated beneath the edges of cliffs and the incautious sportsman in pursuit of his wounded prey may advance a step too far and thus effectually put an end to his adventures for the future. The land shells, chiefly the Heli Arbustorum, that occur about the ruins of the old chapels are looked upon with great veneration by the Shetlander, and are much employed for the cure of disease.

Gloup Voe is certainly one of the wildest and most retired spots in Shetland. The head of the voe is a narrow gorge, and the banks rise precipately on either side to a very considerable height. A small stream steals down the narrow valley and abounds with the finest trout. I was probably the first individual who ever tried fly fishing in its waters. In an hour or so I had caught three dozen of very fair trout and one seatrout, but the burn was at the time very low, and had I tried it after rain my success would probably have been greater. I traced this little streamlet several miles to its source up in the hills, which are I think about the most dismal in Shetland. Hardly a sound is to be heard upon the waste except when the shrill scream of a gull overhead breaks upon the ear, as it bends its airy flight towards some productive fishing station, or the plaintive whistle of the Golden Plover comes from the moss where with a few snipes it breeds, the only inhabitants of this lonesome place.

About the middle of August or often sooner the Golden Plover flock together to the number of fifty or a hundred and retire to the high grounds for the autumn. At this time they afford really good amusement to the sportsman, and are in excellent condition for the table. But they are at the same time shy beyond the power of description, and a sentry of their number is always placed on the highest eminence near their feeding ground, who on the approach of an intruder instantly raises an alarm. He begins with a long, low whistle that the others may be made aware of the danger impending. As you approach nearer he runs about much agitated and when sometimes not more than ten or fifteen yards distant takes to flight, but does not altogether depart, making a small circle around then again alighting at a short distance. Should, however, the sportsman disregard his manoevres and continue to advance towards the main body, he flies off at once in a straight line over the flock, calling them to follow by a shrill and sharp whistle. All then take wing, and leave the disappointed fowler in despair, and the naturalist filled with admiration for their vigilance and instinct.

But alas, too often does the poor sentinel fall a victim to his zealous watch. The excited fowler follows the flock which has settled perhaps some three or four hundred yards from the spot from whence they rose. The watch this time is more careful for his own person, as the fowler seems bent upon destruction. He flies around at a respectful distance, till the patience of the weary fowler is nearly exhausted. Till now he would not think of destroying the sentinel, as his destructiveness would be but poorly gratified by the death of a single bird; or perhaps his ammunition is beginning to fail, and he must be economical of an article so precious up in the hills. But where is he now, the dreaded fowler? He no longer sees him, and he flies to reconnoitre. Alas, he has approached too near the ambushed foe, the gun rings out across the waste, and the poor bird falls with a broken wing. It feebly flutters towards its companions uttering a cry of terror and pain far different from that wherewith it formerly summoned them to seek their safety in flight. The first shock of the wound is past, the maimed bird recovers its strength and runs swiftly over the moss. The fowler much against his will is forced to show himself, and the flock instantly takes to flight. Impatient at his bad success he follows sulkily the poor sentinel, or rather moves in the direction he has gone, for the bird itself is no longer to be seen. He curses the badness of his aim, and after perhaps half an hour's search, the poor creature is found in a peat hag, the blood issuing from its bill which from time to time gapes convulsively, the beautiful dark eyes open and shut, one shiver and the poor watcher ends his existence.

But where is the main flock now? It is late in the afternoon, the sportsman must have more or be content with but poor fare on the morrow. He is a naturalist as well as a pot-hunter, and his game bag is already well filled with Gulls, Terns, Mergansers etc., but none fit for the table save the solitary Golder Plover. He must leave his bag behind if he would follow up his game. A conspicuous hummock is chosen, the bearings of it carefully taken, and having deposited his game bag he sits beside it to look for the Golden Plover. He gives a long, low, melancholy whistle, 'tis repeated three or four times without answer, till at length something like an indistinct echo comes down the wind. He listens with attention, again it strikes upon his ear, and he moves in the direction from whence it came. Cautiously he creeps along, from time to time repeating the signal. And now he can espy the birds. They are all close together on a high peat hag, and as it were entrenched by a ditch at least twelve feet wide on every side. Woe to them, it is the entrenchment that will prove their destruction. Anyone who has travelled over a peat moss willl be aware that the ground is split into a thousand patches by deep water runs, and that these vary in depth according to the inclination of the surface. In Yell, which island is characterised by long, undulating hills with little or no intervening flat land, the water-runs in the peat mosses vary from five to twenty feet in depth, and during the summer months the bottom will support, though barely, the weight of the human body. But to return to the hero of our pen's creating.

His place is already settled, and careful he must be, for by this time other watches have been set from among the birds, and these will be far more wary and vigilant than their predecessors. He slides down into a water-run, the bottom is soft and receives him to the mid-leg. Nothing daunted by so cordial a welcome, he extricates himself quickly and takes down his gun from the grass above, on which he left it for fear of accident in his descent. His position is good, he is on the side of the hill below the plovers, which are feeding quietly at not more than 200 yards' distance. He creeps on in a bending posture for some space, for the sentinels are wary, and constantly change their position to discover the enemy. A single glance of the sun's rays upon the barrel of his gun would be sufficient to scare them all. But a new obstacle presents itself. The run has terminated in a small black pool of water through which he cannot venture to wade. Ascending to the surface of the moss he lays himself flat on the heath, and pushing his gun before him, drags himself thus for two or three yards till he reaches another watercourse. This is deeper than the last, and leads by a tortuous path to the very entrenchment of the plovers. Stealthily he now crawls along, once only, behind some long heather, does he venture to raise his head, and sees the birds still more closely grouped than before. Cautiously and breathless he cocks his gun, fearful lest even that slight sound should betray his approach. But the flock remain perfectly still, and are now within range. He throws his cap on the wet peat-moss, clambers slowly up the bank, the bright barrel is protruded through the heather, and ere the plovers have recovered from the surprise caused by its appearance, four of their number have fallen to the discharge. As they rise, two more are brought down by the second barrel, and the delighted fowler rushes up to secure his prize. The first four are stretched motionless on the heath, but the other two, with broken wings, cost as much trouble in their capture as did the poor sentinel. The joyous sportsman carries them back in triumph to where his game bag is deposited, and the anxiety for the morrow's meal no longer weighs upon his mind.

Such is plover shooting in Yell, and many a time have I gone through this long process almost to its termination and with every hope of immediate success, when the wary sentinel has discovered me as flying over the water-course his shrill cry has been instantly raised, and my night's supper has quickly vanished over the hills.

Gloup Voe is perhaps at this present time one of the best of the fishing stations of Shetland. The fishermen of North Yell are proverbial over the rest of the islands for their daring spirit and recklessness in danger, though in point of superstition they may vie with any people in the world. A Gloup man will never put to sea if the name of the cat, the Devil or the parson has been mentioned in his hearing that morning in good English. Pussy is denominated 'longtail', the respected person second on my list 'Blackman', and the minister goes by the name of the 'upstander'. A knife, a hook, a bundle of lines, in short everything that concerns the fishery, must have its appropriate nickname, and must be spoken of by that name alone.

No life is in my opinion more arduous than that of the fisherman, and particularly of a fisherman in Shetland. During the months of May, June, July and August he rises at one a.m. on the Monday and with a little oatmeal and water for his food, pulls or sails out to the distance of nearly 40 miles from land. Here having performed the heavy task of setting the lines he and his comrades in the boat enjoy a short interval of rest to snatch their miserable meal, and then go to work to take up their lines again. This is by far the hardest task they have to undergo, and feelingly have they often described to me the severity of it. Again the lines are set, again they are hauled up, and should the weather remain favourable they try a third time, and then with light hearts set sail for home. Each expedition to the far Haaf or fishing ground usually occupies from 48 to 60 hours but foul winds and foggy weather will often prolong their absence to three or four days. I have seen the boat of one adventurous fisherman coming into Gloup Voe with over 30 cwt of fish, and the gunnel not then three inches above the water. In this overloaded state the boat had come over 40 miles for they had been to the far side of the far Haaf. Magnus Williamson the skipper of this boat is well known at the Gloup Haaf for his daring spirit and success in fishing and his crew moreover are some of the best oarsmen in Shetland. He himself is a genuine aboriginal, sharp and inquisitive, though generally a month or two behind with his politics, but that is not to be wondered at, as the newspapers are often a good six weeks old ere they reach him. His long curly reddish hair falls down in patriarchal style upon his shoulders, and his caldskin dress suits well his square-built figure. It is with regret that I state, that while staying at the hospitable mansion of Mr Cheyne of Ollaberry in 1834, poor Magnus Williamson came over from Gloup in great tribulation having lost in one stormy night the whole of his lines. This is by far the greatest misfortune that can accrue to the fisherman, as the boats themselves are in general the property of the landholders.

Monday July 30th. Went out about 10 a.m. to shoot Plovers on the hills to the south of Gloup. Killed four and two Snipe, the latter appear to be larger and lighter coloured than those of England. Also shot a Whimbrel or two and hunted the wild sheep with our dog Oscar. I never saw any animals so swift or so active over broken ground, and on the cliffs of the sea shore they appeared as much at home as a Welsh goat on Snowdon. White wooled sheep are rare, most of those in Yell, where the genuine Shetland breed is to be found in its greatest purity, are black and white or spotted of a lighter red, but the prevailing colour is certainly the 'moorit' or a piebald mixture of bluish brown and white. The diminutive size of this pretty animal renders it, no doubt, valueless for the southern market, but the mutton, like that of Wales, is deliciously sweet, and in summer a leg of lamb has but very little more upon it than the similar limb of a turkey. In fact I have myself demolished one at breakfast without any extraordinary appetite.

Wednesday August 1st. About midday we pulled out of the bay voe of Gloup in a small boat or whilly for the holms. The Holms of Gloup are two high isolated rocks which stand out in the sea about half a mile from the coast. There are few holms in Shetland more exposed than these. In the calmest weather a tremendous surge breaks upon their rugged sides which boldly withstand the whole force of the open Atlantic. But exposed as they are, no holms in Shetland afford better pasturage for sheep. The poor animals are conveyed here in calm weather in a boat, and are hauled up by ropes to the top of the holm or else carried on the back of a man up a path which no Southron would attempt to climb in his sober senses. On the north-eastern cliff the Sea Eagle has long had his eyrie, and I was solemnly assured by the people of Gloup that although the finest lambs in Shetland were to be found on their holm, yet that the eagle always sought his prey from the mainland, and left untouched those which had been in a manner confided to his protection.

Upon these isolated rocks sea birds of all kinds are to be met with in the greatest abundance. On the south-eastern side at the bottom of a deep and narrow gio which will barely admit a boat to pass to its farther extremity, is situated the Doo cave, so named from the great quantity of wild pigeons which breed within its recesses. The length of the cave may be 150 or 200 paces, 40 or 60 in height and breadth. Like the gio by which you arrive at it, it is evidently formed by the disintegration of a huge vein of granite, whose smaller branches may still be seen ramifying in all directions in the surrounding strata of gneiss. We entered the cave by a narrow and low aperture, all at first was still and silent, but in a few seconds the rushing sounds of numerous pinions announced that the scared feathered inhabitants were hurrying from the cave. On every ledge we discovered some of the nests of the Rock Dove and we brought away a good supply of their beautifully white eggs.

NOTES:

1   Charlton touches on the later history of Mr Hay in his journal for July 5th, 1852.

2   The author and, presumably, the Hendersons of Gloup on Yell and the Camerons of Unst.

3   Shooting, fishing, botany, ornithology, geology and archaeology.

Shetland 1832

Scenes in North Shetland

[Charlton remained at Gloup for another week, and then he and John Henderson travelled round the northern parts of Shetland, visiting Fetlar, Unst and Northmavine, till the end of September.]

TUESDAY August 7th. Long and tiresome was the delay in cleaning our guns and packing ammunition etc., before we departed for Fetlar. We left the house in company with the ladies but feeling little inclined to regulate our pace by their slow rate of progress, we pushed on to Pole's at Cullivoe and soon engaged a boat with four men to row us to Fetlar. As the day was extremely calm a large six-oared boat was unnecessary, and we crossed the six miles of sea between Cullivoe and Fetlar in a small whilly. When four men pull in a whilly, it is generally arranged that one pulls the two stroke oars (as they are termed in Shetland), and the two others sit on the aftermost bank together, while the fourth man steers the boat and occasionally takes his turn at the oars.

We landed at Urie on the western coast of the island and then engaged a lad to carry our luggage to Jerome Johnstone's house at Corbister near the centre of Fetlar. He led us by an uninteresting pathway but very rugged withal to the house we were in search of, which was certainly much superior in neatness, even externally, to those in its immediate neighbourhood. Mr Johnstone was not at home and his servants seemed to understand but little about the entertainment of strangers. We deposited our luggage in the house, sent back the guide, and then strolled through some very highly cultivated ground to the beach of Town on the south-eastern side of the island. The minister Mr Watson of Yell comes once or twice a month to the church of Town, as the stipend is too small to support a resident pastor. The consequence has been that in this island as in many others more than half the population has gone over to the Methodists who of course are ready to receive them. And really the labours of these men deserve attention as compared with the supine neglect of the Establishment.

The name of Fetlar is said to be derived from Feide Oe or the 'green island'. The valley of Town may vie in richness with that of Tingwall on the mainland. It is covered by nearly an equal quantity of corn and meadow land, the size of the patches of either nowhere exceeding four or five acres. The corn grown here is, I believe, the white bearded oat and the common barley, which seems to flourish here as well as in the south of Scotland. The beach of Town lies at the head of Triesta Bay; we carefully examined its ample extent of sand but no new or rare shells presented themselves to our longing eyes.

We returned very hungry to Corbister where Mr Johnstone awaiting us gave us a hearty welcome and a mighty bowl of porridge for supper, after which we drew our chairs to the fire and introducing a fourth friend in the shape of the whisky bottle we made ourselves most comfortable for the evening. As the conversation proceeded I was surprised to find that Jerome Johnstone had been long in Egypt with the British army and that he could moreover give a most excellent description of the countries he had visited. His narratives were interspersed with various Godly sayings, which carried me back to the days of the old Scottish Covenanters; but the Shetlanders are particularly prone to use such phrases, as 'Wi' God's hjalp' 'He abjuv will guide wis.' Jerome was certainly, however, no Covenanter, but he had far more interest in my eyes as being one of the old udallery of Shetland, a class of men likely in a few years to become totally extinct. Jerome's cottage was small but clean and he accommodated us with a comfortable bed.

Saturday August 11th. At an early hour we left Corbister and proceeded to Urie to embark for the island of Unst. Before we parted Jerome Johnstone presented me with a specimen of the Pinna Ingens which though sadly broken was at that time to me a mighty treasure. I also procured a specimen of the double edged stone axe or steinbarte – a sketch of one may be seen in Hibbert. The minerals I had collected were stowed away in small baskets or capies, which are really of excellent workmanship. At Urie we fell in with Mr W Johnson, a former prisoner aboard the *Magnus Troil*, and as we looked again upon our floating prison then lying about 100 yards from the shore we poured down copious libations to her prosperous voyage to the south. We then pulled off for Unst in a small whilly, and a fine old fisherman with a most patriarchal beard wished us good luck as we left. He was the only Shetlander I ever met with who retained this noble appendage, so honoured by our Scandinavian forefathers. We soon reached the island of Unst whose rocky shores were disagreeably contrasted with the green banks of Fetlar that we had left behind. We directed our course towards Belmont, the residence of Captain Cameron, and on rounding the point east of the house we perceived his daughters standing upon the extreme point of the rock, and looking in an anxious manner in the direction of the *Magnus Troil*. We had kept so close in shore to avoid the tide running out of Blomel Sound that we were close upon them ere they perceived us, and after a hearty welcome we learned that Mr Deans had just gone off to the *Magnus* to persuade, if he could, the captain to remain at Uyea until Monday. The house of Belmont is well and substantially built, but like all in Shetland it is without pretensions to architectural beauty. Mr Deans returned in the evening, a right merry party did we form; the night was terminated with a dance wherein we figured in our shooting jackets with much eclat. I left my packages of minerals on the beach all night, being quite sure that no Shetlander would carry away a parcel of 'chuckie stanes'.

Sunday August 12th. At an early hour the ladies went off to church upon their ponies, each ornamented with its peg and tether, done up in a neat knot upon its shoulder. I remained at home to write letters, and in the evening walked to the hill on the south west of the house where the young ladies in true norse fashion were erecting a cairn to Mr Deans's memory, though their hero had neither departed out of this life not out of the country.

Monday August 13th. At half past five a.m. the signal was flying from the *Magnus Troil* for Mr Deans to repair on board. A most tender parting took place between the old gentleman and the young ladies, and then the schooner bore away for the south. Shortly after we engaged a boat to convey us to Cullivoe. On our way thither we passed through Blomel Sound, wherein runs on of the strongest tides in Shetland. In one part where the water is confined between the north east promontory of Yell and the south west point of Unst the current is at all times so strong that few boats will venture to brave it. Here on the calmest day, when the sea elsewhere was as calm as glass, I have seen the bore, or wall of water, rise several feet in height, and spread on both sides nearly to the shore. At length we arrived at Cullivoe and got to Gloup at 11 a.m. A good deal of coral had been collected by the fisherman during our absence, and from these I selected some very interesting specimens. At night we went out to the hills in search of Red-throated Divers on the lochs, but were unsuccessful save that we filled our bags with Golden Plover.

Wednesday August 15th. After a bathe in the clear waters of Gloup Voe, we started for Cullivoe which we reached at 2 p.m. and immediately engaged a boat to Belmont. As we left I observed a poor ragged looking fellow with a wallet on his back come up to Mr Pole's door. In a few minutes Mr Pole came out with two letters from the south, and which had been brought from Lerwick by this most unobtrusive postman. I was told that he always made his journeys on foot, accomplishing the distance twice a week, and it is at least 50 miles from Unst to Lerwick, by way of Yell and the mainland. We arrived at Belmont in time for dinner

Sunday August 19th. Information was received today that a drove of whales, at least 200 in number, had this morning come into the bay. We hired a small boat from a sloop lying at anchor in the bay and pulled out amongst the whales, which seemed but very little disturbed by our presence. We accordingly walked over about midday and sure enough, as we looked down from the hill above, we could plainly see the monsters tumbling and blowing in its waters. It was indeed a curious and interesting sight to see the great creatures rolling over and over in the bay, at times showing only the back fin, and again raising themselves more than half out of the water. This was the only occasion I ever saw the caaing whale in Shetland. During my stay at Ollaberry in Northmavine intelligence arrived that a drove of 769 whales had been captured on the estate of Mr Bruce near Sumburgh. This was the richest prize that ever fell into the hands of the poor Zetland fishermen.

We hired a small boat from a sloop lying at anchor in the bay and pulled out among the whales, which seemed but very little disturbed by our presence We several times got so near them in our little cock boat that we could have touched them with an oar, and then after a mighty snort they would roll heavily beneath the surface. Their skins like those of the common porpoise were beautifully black and shone like silk. All the inhabitants of Uyea were on the *qui vive*, but the day was sacred, and the religious islander moved his boat, indeed, down to the beach, but dared not launch it on the ocean till the hour of midnight had passed. A few minutes before that time the whales, as though aware that their day of rest was past likewise, moved slowly out of the sound and made for the open sea.

Our little boat glided over the smooth water to the fertile island of Uyea, the property of Mr Leask whose hospitality we were about to claim. Uyea (in Danish an island) is a fair, green island, affording some of the best pasturage in Shetland. Mr Leask's house is situated near the centre of his property, and it presents an appearance of comfort superior to many of the dwellings of the Shetland proprietors. On knocking at the door Mr Leask himself appeared, and the first glance showed that he was no common mortal. Our host stood well above six feet in height, and was apparently approaching his seventieth year, gaunt and bony but with a humorous and somewhat satirical expression of countenance. To describe him from top to toe we must commence with his wig. It was an inimitable affair of the scratch genus, and of a lovely chestnut hue. This pericranial covering sat easy on his reverend head, as it appeared a matter of perfect indifference to the possessor which part of the peruke reposed on his forehead or his occiput. He was clad in a loose blue coat with huge brass buttons, and while this upper garment was a world too wide for his sinewy frame, his trowsers presented a perfect contrast, being below the knee as tight as a dancing master's pantaloons. Mrs Leask was a buxom Dumfriesshire dame from the neighbourhood of Moffat, but having been now many years settled in Uyea, her associations with the South of Scotland were few and far between. We dined with the old gentleman, and right merry was he, for he was full of anecdote relating to the island which he owned, and could tell many a curious tale of other parts of Shetland.

Tuesday September 4th. A heavy storm from the north east, and no hope of crossing Yell Sound[1] while it lasted. At 6 p.m. however the weather had so much moderated that we started in a good six oared boat for North Roe, where we landed at 9 p.m. to the great joy of Henderson, to whom the heavy seas had been anything but agreeable during the transit. Had curdled milk for supper and slept in a garret.

Thursday September 6th. The wind blew very heavily from the south, but we faced the gale in Mr Henderson's boat as far as Colafiord. We arrived there at 2 p.m. and geologised for some hours to our great satisfaction. In coming over the hills towards Ollaberry and when near the chromate mines of Sugon I entered a small cottage and enquired for the ancient Danish stone axes which are known by the name of Thunderbolts. I was fortunate enough to secure two of them, but both were of small size and one was made of a singularly banded quartz rock. We reached Ollaberry at seven p.m. where we were most hospitably received by Mr Cheyne.

Friday September 7th. About midday we crossed the hills to Hillswick Ness, and arrived at the mansion of Hillswick at 3 p.m. It is the residence of Thomas Gifford, a younger brother of Mr Gifford of Busta who had spent the greater part of his life in the East Indies. At seven p.m. Mr Gifford returned from Tangwick accompanied by a young Scotch advocate of the name of Napier who had come to Shetland in search of documents and witnesses in the cause of Mr Gifford of Busta.[2]

Monday September 10th. I was out the whole day upon Hillswick Ness. The immediate vicinity of Hillswick abounds in the most stupendous coast scenery. On the west of the Ness the rocks rise to a great height and are cut down into rugged peaks and precipices by the ceaseless action of the winds and sea. The Ness of Hillswick is a peninsula about two miles in length and seldom more than a quarter of a mile in breadth, jutting out boldly into the bay of St Magnus. Its geological structure is as interesting as its coast scenery. The great tracts of syenetic greenstone on the east, and of granite on the west of Northmavine, are here separated for a space of three or four miles in length, and between these we observe beds of mica and of chlorate slate, with horneblende, traversed by veins of porphyry and abounding in mineral products. These constitute the promontory of Hillswick Ness, and here the wonder-working ocean has gambolled in its wildest mood. The contorted strata of hornebliende have been upheaved and traversed in a hundred different directions by the veins of porphyry, and upon the sea cliffs of the Ness the latter have resisted the action of the waves, while the softer stratified rock has disappeared, and in this way have been formed those pinnacles or 'stacks' which form so conspicuous a feature of Hillswick Ness. Almost all these natural obelisks are composed of the finest close grained felspar porphyry, the basis containing the crystals being either a reddish claystone or more frequently a blue silicious rock, which well deserves the name of Hornstone, and which is found in particular beauty at the Taing of Torness.

The minerals which are met with in this singular formation are numerous and beautiful. At the Queen Gio on the eastern banks are strata of a most beautiful mica slate alternating with quartz and studded with perfectly crystallised garnets of from half an inch to an inch in diameter. A little distance from thence occurs actinolite of a beautiful leek green colour and in masses of large size, while in some specimens the crystals of this mineral are disseminated separately, like those of the Tyrol, in a matrix of pearly talc. At the Gio of Gordiestack on the west chlorite is met with in abundance, with pearly nacrite of a reddish pink hue, and in the chlorite are embedded numerous octohedrons of magnetic iron ore. Close to this spot is a vein of light pistachio green epidote with well defined crystals.

It is on the western side of the promontry that the grandest rock scenery is presented to the eye. The Drongs, a mighty mass of granite, rise between two and three hundred feet from the ocean, at a distance of about half a mile from the shore. Under certain aspects these huge and isolated rocks present the appearance of towers and of a castellated building, while from the north or south, where their sharpened edge is presented to the spectator, they form narrow slender stacks of pinnacles. During the long summer nights, when though the sun has gone down a bright red and yellow sky tinges the north till it melts into the roseate hue of morn, the summits of the Drongs, white with the droppings of innumerable sea fowl, show out like the sails of some huge phantom ship, peering above the mist which at that hour floats lazily and low over the surface of the ocean.

To the north of Hillswick Ness and above the bay immediately west of the church rises a high cliff of red granite. From a spot about a hundred feet from the summit of this precipice there gushes out, especially after long continued rains, a mud spring (if it may be so called) carrying with it a large quantity of red clay intermixed with numerous fragments of felspar. My attendant Laurie Robertson[3] slung himself with a rope over the giddy height to obtain some of this remarkable product, which has long been a subject of wonder to the Shetlanders.

Tuesday September 11th. At six a.m. I set off for Tangwick and reached that hospitable house by seven in good time to breakfast with Mr Cheyne, the brother of the proprietor of Ollaberry. He was dreadfully affected with a violent chronic cough which rendered him at times very difficult to understand. He showed me a curious piece of coral which had lately been brought to him from the Haaf or deep sea fishing, and which bore a rude though striking resemblance to the human face and figure. It was no doubt regarded with awe by the superstitious Shetlanders, who would certainly believe it to be a petrified mermaid or great Sea Trow converted into Cranzie.

From hence I continued my journey to Esha Ness, a station equal in importance to that of Gloup Voe, and then turned northward to seek the Grind of the Navir. Along the whole of the west coast of Northmavine from Stenness to the mouth of Roeness Voe a mural rampart of porphyry bounds the amygdaloid rocks as if to protect the more fragile material from the Atlantic. But at the Grind of the Navir the barrier itself has given way to so mighty an engine of destruction, a passage has been burst in the porphyry wall, which here is at least forty yards in thickness, and the huge ruins strewn beyond the breach attest the power of the conquering element. The word Grind is of Norse extraction and signifies an opening or wicket in a wall, and nowhere is this more applicable than in the present instance. The bed of the breach is by no means on a level with the surface of the ocean, being at least 20 feet above high water mark. What must then be the force of that wave which can tear stones from their position at so great a height and project them some hundred yards upon the plain? But the foundation itself of the Grind is beginning to give way. In 1834 Mr Cholmeley[4] told me he had observed a small hole or funnel on the right side of the Grind, through which, though elevated twenty feet above the ocean level, the waves spouted with great force, and formed a species of marine fountain on a grand scale. I had closely examined all parts of the Grind two years before Cholmeley's visit, and this singular phenomenon, had it then existed, would undoubtedly have attracted my attention.

The whole shore here is pierced with caverns, the rocks are worn into pillars and arches of the most fantastic forms. A little to the south of the Grind of the Navir are the holes of Scradda, a fearful yawning cleft, of whose existence you are not aware till close upon the brink. The sea this day lay calm and still in this inland basin, while not three hundred yards off the ocean, though unseen, roared hoarsely against the rocky barrier. A little before we arrived at the Grind my guide led me to the brink of the precipice, and bade me take off my shoes, in preparation for a climb. He disappeared over the brink, and I followed him down the face of the cliff for about twenty or thirty yards till we stood before the mouth of a cavern. 'This,' said he, 'is the Barn of Scradda; you have heard of it before.' I had; I knew it as one of the great resorts of the hunted natives during the last war, when the pressgangs desolated the country. It was hither that they had often fled, that by their number and by the natural strengh of their position they might bid defiance to the cruelty of the laws. Above them the rock was nearly perpendicular and the greatest care was required in the descent which admitted of but one man at a time, while below at the depth of one hundred feet rolled the dark ocean. The platform before the cave is not more than four feet square, and below that the rock resumes its perpendicularity down to the sea. The cave is not large but dry and comfortable within, and has no doubt been the scene of many a night of anxious misery.

NOTES:

1   They had arrived the previous day at Sandwick on the west side of Yell.

2   In this case, Gifford v. Gifford of Busta, 'a young man educated I believe in America attempted on a plea of bastardy to dispossess the present most honoured proprietor, but his endeavours were eventually futile.' (E.C.)

3   Charlton's journal for July 7th 1852 gives a description of Lawrence Robertson later in life.

4   Charlton's cousin, who accompanied him on his visit in 1834.

Shetland 1832

Departure

FRIDAY September 21st. I remained all day in the house[1] packing till the evening, when I crossed the voe to Westafirth and purchased a lamb of the moorit or brown and white variety for one shilling and sixpence. I wished to take with me to England not only the beautiful natural history productions of these islands but also to carry away whatever was remarkable in the dress of the Shetland people. For this purpose I purchased today from James Moir a skin coat and fishing boots, and procured a pair of breeches, mittens and a nightcap, to render my fishing dress complete. From James Moir I also bought a couple of sealskins at half a crown each, and these now form a comfortable case for my fowling piece. The lamb which I had purchased this morning, I slaughtered this night with my dirk, and laid it by to skin on the following morning. The sealskins that I got were of the common species, the Phoca Vitulina, and I in vain endeavoured while in Shetland to obtain a skin of the Phoca Barbata or Haaf fish.

Saturday September 22nd. I was engaged during the greater part of the morning in skinning and preparing my lamb previous to packing it up. Having accomplished this trifling job, which was however by no means an agreeable one to me, I took my fishing rod, which I had never touched since I came to Shetland, and went to fish at the head of the voe.[2]

Lectori benevolo! Here my journal breaks off and at the distance of ten years I can recall to mind but little of what passed from this day till my final departure from Shetland on the tenth of October. My heavy luggage was transported to Cullivoe in Mr Pole's boat and there on a subsequent day, I think the 29th of September, I joined the *Magnus Troil* and with William Cameron sailed for Ollaberry. Here we once more fell in with our kind entertainer Mr Cheyne, and after touching at Mossbank we landed at Lerwick. Here I found Mr Henderson, and we again took up our residence under the hospitable roof of Mr Hay. From the second of October the *Magnus Troil* was ready for sea, we were detained by a strong and steady south wind until the tenth of that month. During this long period I managed to employ myself in geologising the neighbouring country, but my excursions were always limited by the fear that the wind might change in my absence. I walked one day over to Scalloway and slept at the house of Mr Scott, another day I was at Gardie, and upon the 9th I set off for the island of Noss. I left Lerwick at 7 a.m. and continued my excursion till six or seven p.m. when I returned greatly fatigued and I am sorry to say somewhat elated by an old witch's potations administered to me in the island of Bressay.[3] The wind had changed during my absence and I narrowly escaped being left behind. The next morning we were afloat and at six a.m. moved out of the harbour. There was a motley crew on board, sundry merchants from Lerwick, and half a dozen sailors from the Greenland seas, who were returning to Leith after having lost their ship and barely saved their lives in those inhospitable seas. They were however a merry and careless set, and had rigidly adhered to the ancient maritime custom of enjoying themselves on shore, as they were all more or less intoxicated when they came on board.

The morning was fine but there was a very heavy ground swell setting in from the south east, the quarter from which the wind had blown persistently during the last fortnight. I had been sick enough when I rose in the morning on dry land, from the potations of the previous evening, but now a calm, seconded by a ground swell such as this, when the topmasts of the ships in company were at times scarcely visible, effectually discompassed my inward man, and I was sea-sick again and for the last time. I had always been a pretty good and hearty sailor in this respect, and for two years before this time had become so inured to the motion of the waves when shooting on the Firth of Forth that the thought of being affected by them seldom entered my mind. We made but little way all day and at night were still off the coast. The next evening we passed the Fair Isle, and the wind began to freshen. This day I had been quite well, and indeed I was quite revived the day before by a huge plate of boiled beef and potatoes which I managed to dispose of while sitting in my berth. I was busily engaged all this day in studying the management of the ship, and at night I retired to my berth with my head stuffed full of nautical terms, added to a good supper and an abundant supply of grog. O what delicious pleasure did I take in annoying one Gilbert Robertson, a shopkeeper of Lerwick, who had been the foremost of the opponents during the quarantine. I saw that he was dreadfully afraid of the disorder, and did all in my power to add to his terrors by the most harrowing descriptions of its ravages. But the next morning brought other topics of conversation. About 4 a.m. I was awakened by the violent motion of the ship, and by shouts upon deck with the trampling of many feet overhead. Chairs, hats and coats were dancing about the cabin, and I was soon painfully convinced of the propensity of motion imparted to everything by my provision of ship's biscuit and butter, which I had taken to bed, as was my custom, and which saw daylight again, leaping out of my bunk. I could hear the heavy seas roaring as they advanced against the ship, and then there was a kind of pause, and then a shock which almost tossed me up against the top of my berth. After this there was another calm, and then there came three or four such rude shocks in succession, and at the conclusion of these like rain after thunder, the briny flood poured along the decks, and fell drip, drip down the companion ladder. Luckily all appeared to be well made fast on deck, and I lay wondering how they could manage to cook the beef steaks for breakfast, when after a heavier sea than usual I heard an outcry on deck, and as it passed along I thought it signified the boom was carried away. This was awful news indeed for to that identical spar was appended a magnificent piece of beef, from whence were to be derived the juicy steaks for breakfast and for dinner I had been anticipating. I jumped out of my bunk and into my clothes without being once capsized, and found my way to the door and up the companion ladder, and then watching my opportunity took advantage of a lull to open one door of the narrow hatchway and to get out upon deck. It was a wild scene indeed. With the exception of the mate who was at the wheel, with another man to aid him, the whole of the crew were forward on the bowsprit, from which I saw the jibboom had been carried away a few minutes before. This loss they were endeavouring to repair and first and foremost in the perilous task was the Captain, James Ganson. As I came up the mate cried to me to keep below as it was 'no weather for a gentleman to be upon the deck'. But I delighted in remaining and watched with the keenest pleasure the wild motion of the storm. Danger there was little or none, the sea broke furiously over us, but not so as to require that we should lash ourselves to anything to avoid being carried overboard. At breakfast and at dinner there was a miserable muster, and I spent the evening for want of better society among the jolly tars in the forecastle. And a merry night we made of it.

The next day we ran past Stonehaven, the Bell Rock and the May, and off the Bass picked up a pilot who proved to be my old boatman John Seaton. We ran into Leith roads that night and the next morning I found my way, somewhat unsteadily at first after the motion of the ship, along Leith walk up to Edinburgh where I arrived safe back at my lodgings on the 14th of October 1832 after an absence from Scotland of somewhat more than three months.

NOTES:

1   Gloup, to which he had returned on the 18th.

2   See above, p. 28

3   Details of this incident are given in Charlton's journal for June 16th 1834.

Shetland 1834

Outward journey to Vaila

MY former visit to Shetland had left so many lively and agreeable impressions on my mind that I resolved to revisit that country in the summer of 1834. My cousin Henry Cholmeley[1] offered to accompany me as the sporting naturalist or fowler to the expedition. I also engaged Mr Procter of the Durham Museum, whom I had long known as a most zealous naturalist and an admirable auxiliary in these wild enterprises. Early in June Procter arrived in Edina, and the 10th of the month was the day on which we were to sail.

Tuesday June 10th. We came down yesterday to sail, but the ship either could not or would not go out on the afternoon tide. After seeing all our effects safely stowed in the hold, we resolved not to return to Edinburgh as the laugh would be so dreadfully against us for our precipitation. To kill time we visited the glass works at the back of Leith Pier and then returned to sleep on board of the *Magnus Troil* about 9 p.m. The cabin was as close as a glasshouse and, the rain continuing to fall heavily all the evening, it was impossible to remove the skylight.

Wednesday June 11th. At four a.m. we were all aroused by the heavy tramping of many feet upon the deck. I found that we had recommenced our voyage which yesterday had only extended the length of the dock, and that we were then passing through the dock gates. 'Well, we are now fairly off' thought I. Having passed through the dock gates, the ship was hauled alongside of the pier to wait for Dr Cowie[2] and some other passengers, the pilot reassuring us that we had got thirteen feet of water. Dr Cowie not appearing, the sails were loosed, and we prepared to move fairly out of the harbour. But alas, we had already arrived at the terminus of that morning's voyage, the vessel obeyed not the summons to move, for she was immovably fixed in the mud, there to be till the afternoon's tide. Great indeed was the wrath of the Captain at the stupidity of the pilot, who had assured him of thirteen feet of water when there was in reality hardly eight. We could not stay another day in Leith, so resolved to return to Edinburgh and brave all the laughter our misfortune would be sure to incite. At four p.m. we returned to the *Magnus Troil* which was just leaving the pier as we jumped on board, but Dr Cowie and two others were left in Leith. Much to the pleasure of the Captain these individuals had to follow us in a boat, paying, of course, a heavy fare as the price of their delay.

Thursday June 12th. What a glorious tossing did we endure throughout the night in crossing the Bay of St Andrews, and this morning the fair breeze has blown its last, and we are rocking to and fro on the glassy ocean. Poor Cholmeley! It is all up with him in this deuced calm, the groanings and heavings of his inward man quite equal those of the ship timbers. Oh the horrors, to landsmen and to sailors, though for widely different reasons, of a dead calm at sea, with a nice swell heaving on your broadside to teach you civilly to exchange plates at dinner with your neighbour, or to deposit at breakfast your cup of coffee on the lap of your *vis a vis*.

Friday June 13th. The young lad who officiates as steward on board sprained his ankle severely last night, and implored the medical aid of Dr Cowie. In joke this worthy disciple of Aesculapius tied round the wounded part a 'breisten thread' or a string with a mystic number of knots upon it, and therewith enjoined that cold water *ad libitum* should be poured on the joint, and that the limb should be kept perfectly quiet. The magic thread has worked with wondrous power, and it would be a pity to undeceive the lad by ascribing all its effects to the rest and to the cold water affusions. About six p.m. when we were about sixty miles from any land a huge finner whale rose quite under the stern of the vessel, as I was leaning over the bulwarks, and curving his back into a graceful arch, rolled down again into the deep. From the size of his back fin, the sailors said that he could not be less than 60 or 70 feet in length.

[The *Magnus Troil* reached Lerwick on the 14th, and the passengers landed without formalities. Although Charlton's main intention was to visit the western islands of Foula and Papa Stour, he and his companions remained at Lerwick until the 20th, making day trips from the town to collect specimens of insects and birds.]

Monday June 16th. At seven o'clock we set off in high spirits for the island of Noss, but the wind was east and the sea was consequently too heavy to allow of our going thither in a boat. We resolved therefore to walk over the island of Bressay and take what shooting we could get by the way. We landed at a small gio near the church of Bressay, and as soon as we got on shore we loaded our guns. I must not forget that we were this day accompanied by Peter Williamson, the person with whom we lodged in Lerwick, and in true Lerwick fashion he shut up his shop for the day and trudged away with us to the hills, carrying a huge gun or rather musket of antique fashion. 'Slow and sure' should have been the name of this ancient weapon, for *slow* enough it was in the explosion, and *sure* enough too, if you but aimed well, to carry many feet wide of the mark. Having invaded the school and carried off one of the student boys to be the carrier of my rifle we struck straight across the island in the direction of Noss.

As we came down the banks of the narrow sound which separates the island of Bressay from that of Noss, the shrill pipe of the Oyster-Catcher resounded along the shore. Away went Procter and Cholmeley, the former wanted specimens, the latter wanted sport, and while the boatman was getting ready at the ferry they fired three or four times, yet scatheless flew the beautiful sea pie over my head. With all my veneration for this persecuted bird, I could not resist firing in my turn, yet still unharmed he flew on and I thought myself or my gun assuredly bewitched. On a sudden it struck me that I was in the immediate neighbourhood of the veriest witch in all Shetland, and assuredly had she lived a century ago she would have been sentenced like poor Marian Pardon to be 'wysit till ane staike and brynt til deid.' I half expected as I looked round to see the old hag at her door muttering incantations dire against those who dared to trouble and massacre her familiar spirits, like the Lapland witches so feelingly dwelt upon by old Knud Leoms. Betty Yorston sells wine to the sailors, and many a crown has she received from the superstitious ships' captains as they touched at Brassay on their way to the Greenland seas. O! Betty Yorston! Most dangerous witch thou art, hast thou forgotten the dinner, of three half boiled potatoes and a pint of whisky, that you gave me two years ago? For then you bewitched *me too*, and to this day I know not whether I walked or swam or sailed across to Bressay Sound that night. Six glasses of whisky unless the potion were drugged indeed could never have produced such an effect upon a fasting man!

At length our boat was ready and we crossed the narrow sound, through which a strong tide continually runs, and raises a high sea in the very calmest weather. The island of Noss is of very small extent but affords excellent pasturage for sheep. It formerly abounded in rabbits which were still very numerous when I before visited this spot, but they are now nearly exstirpated. The western side opposite to Bressay is low and sandy while to the east it rises suddenly to a height of 400 to 500 feet. We ascended the Noup[3] of Noss by its northern side, by the edge of a tremendous precipice which grew more deep and and more fearful as we mounted higher. The face of the rock beneath us was covered with innumerable sea birds, though from the crumbling state of the 'banks' we could not in many places venture near enough to inspect them. Half way up the Noup a Peregrine Falcon flew out from her eyrie a foot or two below us and filled the air with wild cries. In vain did I wait, lying down on the bare rock for her return. She flew in wide circles over my head, always keeping out of gunshot, and screaming louder and louder when I moved from my position. In a short time we all stood upon the summit of the Noup, and looked down upon the ocean 500 feet below. Here as in Foulah the lower edges of this magnificent precipice are tenanted by the Shags, Razorbills and Guillemots, while the Puffins, Herring Gulls and Lesser Black Backed Gulls occupy the higher portion of the cliff. The entire height is estimated at 484 feet above the level of the sea, which though lower by 1000 feet than the cliffs of Foulah presents from its great perpendicularity a most imposing effect.

Descending from thence we soon arrived opposite the famous Holm of Noss, of which I have seen many representations, but not one the least like the original. All of them err in placing the Holm too insulated, and making it at the same time much too high. The engraving in Hibbert's *Shetland* is the most faithful of any, though but a miserable specimen of the graver's art. The Holm, in fact, instead of projecting boldly into the sea is rather encased among the surrounding rocks, yet between them there is a chasm of frightful depth. The herring gulls and the great black backed gulls now hold undisputed possession of the Holm, for some malicious fool has cut the ropes on the landward side, and the remains of them were plainly to be seen hanging down the opposite rock. The expense of a new set of ropes is considerable, and it is not at present the intention of the owner, Mr Mouat of Garth, to replace them. These ropes, I am sorry to say, were found cut the day after the Englishmen had visited the island of Noss, and really I do not believe that any of the inhabitants would have been guilty of so mean an action.[1]

Everyone has heard of the cradle of Noss, and of the circumstances under which it was first slung across the gulf. A Foulah man, induced by the tempting offer of a cow, first accomplished this perilous understaking. He climbed up the north side of the Holm, carrying along with him two large stakes to fix in the ground at the summit, and from the moment he first set foot thereon, the undivided empire of the *Gulls* was at an end. But they enjoyed a terrible revenge. The daring rockman refused to return by the rational mode of the basket, but insisted on descending by the way that he came, and in the attempt, as might be expected, he fell and was dashed to atoms. But the cradle was slung every year, and the Holm frequently visited, sometimes to place a few sheep thereon to crop its rich rank herbage, or again for the sake of the eggs of the sea fowl, and lastly by the bold and adventurous, to prove the strength of their nerves.

Wednesday June 18th. We set out about seven for a loch on the hills where the Black-throated Diver is said to breed. Passing Sound we left the road to Scalloway on our right, and so arrived at a small lake, but not a living creature was seen upon its surface. We shot a few Golden Plovers on the hills around, and then turned to the South, towards the Loch of Brinnastir. On a holm in the centre of the large sheet of water the Black-backed Gull breeds in apparent security, nestling amidst the ruins of an ancient burgh which can easily be seen from the shore. From the loch we proceeded too the town of Brinnastir, a town being, as every Scotchman knows, only a farmhouse or homestead. In Shetland it seems also to mean the land lying round a cluster of houses. Entering a small hovel, though a dwelling of the better sort, we were hospitably welcomed to Shetland by the owner, and in right ancient Hialtlandic fashion 'efter gamte skik' he set before us a jug of Bland with Bannocks, sweet milk and Bursten Broonies.

Here! I am sure the reader is brought to a full stop by the mention of all these unheard of delicacies. Bland is a thin, sharp drink prepared by pouring hot water on the buttermilk as soon as the butter is taken out, and it is then set aside until fermentation to a slight degree has taken place. In three or four days it is fit for use. For my part I am extravagantly fond of this beverage, and perhaps not a little on account of its being used in time long gone by as the general drink of the northern nations, and to this day Bland is to be met with in every farm house in Iceland.

But if this dainty beverage excite not the reader's thirst, of a certainty he will hunger sorely on ruminating over the description of that *summum bonum* the 'Bursten Broonie'. And here will I generously present him with a receipt for the compounding thereof. Take of the coarsest Shetland oatmeal, ground in a genuine Shetland watermill,⁵ and not afterwards sifted, two good gowpens or handfuls. Add of water *quantum suff.* till it sticks well together. Make it then into a round cake, three inches in diameter by two in depth, put it then into the hot turf ashes, till it is thoroughly done on the outside. Then withdraw it, and on breaking the cake there will forthwith rush out a most savoury steam, which you must check unstinted by a large lump of butter, and then eat cautiously for fear of swallowing too much sand at a mouthful, or lest you break a tooth upon a fragment of the millstone. Such is a Bursten Broonie.

Cholmeley had left us for a few minutes to procure some snipes in a meadow, and we wound our way down to the water's edge, where, seeing a boat, we resolved to return by water to Lerwick. We soon engaged a boatman, a perfect Hercules, six feet two at the least, and altogether a most noble specimen of the Shetlander. We proceeded to the banks of the voe, to a little cove wherein his boat was drawn up on the beach. How often have I thought of the clear deep blue water of this lovely cove where the rocks went sheer down on every side save one, where a sparkling bed of white sand seemed placed here to invite the bather into crystal water. I was greatly interested by the boatman, who seemed to possess a great fund of good sense, yet he was as unpolished and unsophisticated as an Icelander. Everything we possessed was to him a matter of novelty, and he was not like the proud Highlander ashamed to acknowledge himself ignorant of their use. His long hair hung in elf locks over his shoulders, escaping in abundance from beneath his red cap, which marked him as the father of a family. He said he was happy and contented and did not care much for seeing other climes, for, added he, 'Heir haw we ta trui lest o ta gospell'. Nothing excited his curiosity more than our percussion double barrelled guns, for till this day he had never seen anything but single flints.

> [On Thursday the 19th, the party 'purchased some biscuits, rum and whiskey [*sic*] to support us in Foulah, for the necessities even of life are scarce enough in that remote island'. Their plan was to cross from Vaila Sound on the most westerly coast of the mainland, and for the first part of their journey there, from Lerwick to Scalloway, they hired three ponies.]

Friday June 20th. At half past four this morning we were roused by the lad with the ponies, and having seen our luggage, trunks, bags and boxes safely stowed away, we again retired to rest till near seven, when Cholmeley awoke us, and having breakfasted we started for Scalloway over a road well known as one of the most dismal and most uninteresting in Shetland.

But think not, gentle reader, that I speak here of a noble turnpike, smooth as a bowling green and hard as adamant withal. Turnpike road here there is none, bye road here there is none, horse road there is none, no! indeed there is scarcely a vestige of a track, it is all jump, jump, from one peat hag to another, till you arrive in sight of the castle of Scalloway, the monument of the tyranny of Earl Patrick Stuart.

At Scalloway we breakfasted on cold piltocks, the young of the Dethe or Coalfish, and we all agreed in pronouncing them to be a great delicacy. Here we hired a boat to convey us to Vailley [Vaila] Sound, the residence of Mr Scott, and which we hoped to reach at an early period in the afternoon if the tide would favour us in rounding Skelda Ness. We started in a stout six-oared Norway yawl which, propelled by four active Scalloway men, carried us rapidly through the beautiful archipelago of islands in the bay. We passed far clear of a small sloop which lay out at some distance from the shore, and which by a curious stretch of authority had been put in quarantine for having a few cases of typhus fever on board. In a short time we arrived at Papa Little,[6] the island in which the junction of the epidotic syenite with the gneiss is beautifully seen. I worked long and arduously with my heavy hammer at the former of these rocks ere I could procure even a decent specimen, for in toughness it is exceeded only by the diallage of Baltic Sound and the hypersthene of Cornisk in Skye.

While I was busily engaged with these rebellious rocks, Procter had wandered off to the west end of the island to search for the Stormy Petrels which are said to breed here in considerable numbers. A young man of almost Herculean frame came up to me while I was working at the epidotic syenite. From his begrimed and sooty visage, the finely developed right arm and above all from the knowing way in which he handled my tools, I knew him to be a blacksmith, but of what use that trade would be in this almost uninhabited island, I acknowledge, is yet to remain a subject of conjecture. I questioned him about Stormy Petrels. 'Oh ya! ta mooties, tamm, we will fin dem suin', and away I went with him, and we found Procter gazing listlessly on the blue ocean in utter despair of obtaining the object of his search. We roused him from his reverie and our guide led him to the shore, where masses of sea-borne stones lay piled in hideous confusion. He bade us now be silent for an instant, and we listened with breathless attention. 'Dere is ane doon hier' said he, bending over the stone on which he stood. I approached and heard a low purring noise which seemed to issue from the very bowels of the earth. To work we went, turning over with surprising execution the mighty stones, till in a few minutes our guide, thrusting his hand beneath a half-raised rock, brought out in triumph a little struggling Stormy Petrel. How did the face of Procter beam with joy at this unexpected good fortune, and sadly did he moralise over the poor creature's melancholy fate, whilst he held it a prisoner in his hand. But did he let it go?[7]

The quantity of oil the little creature spurted from his nostrils was indeed surprising and our guide earnestly entreated us not to allow any of it to fall upon my hands or face, assuring me that it was a most deadly poison. Let me not smile too readily at this harmless delusion, for daily do we, in our own educated land, meet with individuals of the middle, nay even of the higher ranks, who talk seriously of the venom of the toad.

Leaving Papa we sailed to the north west past Hildasay (Hilda's Island) till we arrived at a small low rock called Scourholme. Our boatmen now, to our great disappointment, informed us that the tide and wind were too strong against us to pull around Skelda Ness, and therefore proposed to land us at Raewick, whence we could easily get our luggage over land to Vailley Sound. There was no alternative, so leaving on our right Bigsetter Voe we pulled round a point of granite rock into the harbour of Raewick and landed on a beach of fine sand below the house of Mr Garrick. Our luggage was put on shore, the boatmen received the fare and immediately pushed off again to avail themselves of the strong tide running into the Bay of Scalloway.

Here then we stood with all our heavy luggage upon the sand, wondering greatly how we should ever get it conveyed across the hills to Vailley Sound. It was, however, an easy task to procure carriers for our things. A woman and two boys immediately offered themselves, but at the same time somewhat damped our hopes by assuring us that it was six good Shetland miles to Vailley Sound. We now proceeded to divide our luggage, and each took as much as he thought he could conveniently carry. Procter took my gun case with the two heavy geological hammers and a large bag of swan shot; on the top of all he slung his own carpet bag. The woman, a stout Shetland dame of mature years, brought from her house a capie or straw basket, into which she put Cholmeley's carpet bag, a heavy bag full of minerals, my own botanical apparatus and two stones of shot. The strongest of the two lads had Procter's large deal box on his shoulders and beside this a bag full of shot as ballast; and the younger boy was somewhat overloaded by my leather trunk. Cholmeley took charge of my weighty rifle and of Procter's barrelled gun, and bore besides another stone of shot. My own load was small, three boat cloaks, two guns and two shot belts, but the cloaks annoyed me sadly by their unweildy size.

At starting we all felt considerably wearied, having eaten nothing since nine a.m., and it was now six in the evening. As we advanced, however, upon the desolate moor, and gained the higher grounds, our spirits rose and I amused myself, loaded as I was, with shooting Golden Plovers, of which birds we met with several large flocks. Our burdens became truly oppressive, in fact, to use a racing phrase, we were all overweighted, and often did we call a halt to rest and to allow time for the stragglers to come up. In order to accomplish this with the greatest possible comfort, we found a convenient peat hag, and then slipping down its yielding sides into its still more yielding bottom of black moss, we rested our shoulders and the heavy burdens they bore against the top of the bank. It this position the greater part of our bodies were concealed, and it was curious enough when gazing over the wide waste to see nought save six heads, appearing at very considerable distances from each other upon the desolate moor. We straggled miserably apart, and

I blush to record that the woman was generally the foremost of the party. On we toiled on moss and moor and holt and hill, till the welcome sight of a long voe stretching inland told us that our toils were drawing to an end. We began speedily to descend from the high grounds, the declivity was occasionally very steep, and the loads pressed doubly heavy on our galled shoulders. Right glad was I, when on surmounting the long low hill, we espied a voe close beneath our feet, and I was sure it was the one on whose waters we soon should be embarked.

Close below the little eminence on which we stood was a town, a scattered town, indeed, of homely edifices, and to the nearest house we turned our steps. It was the abode of a blacksmith, one of a numerous fraternity in Shetland; we bowed low (to save our heads from encountering the doorway) and entered Vulcan's dwelling. In true old Norse fashion the entry was through the cow byer, steaming and redolent of ought but sweets, and from thence we were ushered into the hall of dais, into the sanctum of the edifice. The 'riggin' was above our heads, but a bare riggin we could not term that which was incrusted with at least three inches of soot. Chimney, of course, there was none. An opening in the centre of the roof, immediately above the fire, allowed of the egress of the smoke and admitted light enough to see one's way in the apartment. The smithy was at the other end of the house and the doorway was guarded by two young calves, which in the smoke and darkness Procter mistook for two huge mastiffs. Around the fire were arranged soft seats of turf for the family, and above them were piled chests, skin coats, dried fish etc., in endless confusion. The old man himself, a stout and hearty Shetlander, soon appeared with a bowl of bland which we eagerly drained, and then longed to drink again.

We soon bargained for a boat to Vailley, and having dismissed our crew of porters with the quantity of a shilling a head, we descended to the shore, and were soon on a most beautiful summer's eve gliding over the smooth waters of the voe. On our way down the inlet we passed a sloop coming in from the cod fishery, with 700 cod on board; the crew were all in high glee, and celebrated with loud songs and hurrahs the good success that had attended their labours. This year 1834 the sloop had been exceedingly successful, but for many previous seasons it had been in a languishing state. But this year the small boat fishery had produced little or nothing, so that the gain for the few proprietors of the sloops will be very great indeed.

It was now about nine p.m. Twelve hours had elapsed since we had tasted food, and faint, cold and hungry were we indeed. as we stepped on the beach in front of the hospitable house of Mr Scott of Melby.[8] I immediately took up a letter to Mr Scott which had been given me by Mr Charles Ogilvy of Lerwick, The introduction was unnecessary. I was met upon the staircase by a gentleman apparently of about fifty years of age, though I had been given to understand that Mr Scott was in his eightieth year. Impressed with this idea I half hesitated ere I gave him the letter. He smiled, perhaps he guessed the cause of my delay, but in a few minutes all our luggage was brought up into a bedroom, and we ourselves were installed before a blazing fire in a well furnished apartment. Supper was hastily prepared, and stout indeed may have been our digestive organs to have submitted with a good grace to a meal of thick, ropy sour cream with hard boiled eggs and oatcake, and the whole commenced and concluded with a dram of genuine Hollands. Having finished our repast, we adjourned to rest, and to our astonishment our couch was a noble feather bed, too soft, almost, for those who at the best had enjoyed nothing but a straw mattress for the last fortnight.

Saturday June 21st. Procter was busily employed today in skinning and setting up the Stormy Petrels we had yesterday obtained in Papa Little. The best mode of preserving these greasy little birds is to stuff them completely at once, while the skins are fresh, although this process of course occupies a great deal of that time which is so valuable on these excursions. The wind blew today from the south west, so that though by no means strong it was directly opposed to our proceeding to Foulah, a circumstance which I did not much regret as we all required repose after yesterday's fatigues. I employed myself in writing my journals and finishing a few sketches.

Sunday June 22nd. The morning was cloudy, and a heavy sea rolled into Vailley Sound from the west, and gave us but indifferent hopes of reaching Foulah on the morrow. About midday I made a tour of the island with its most worthy proprietor, and meeting Procter on my return, we started together to make the circuit of the sea-girt isle a second time. Finding on the south side a pretty good descent among the rocks we scrambled from one steep to another, till the bare and ragged rock frowned over us above, and at the perpendicular depth of two or three hundred feet rolled the wild and stormy Atlantic. We proceeded on till we were fairly involved among the precipices. Return we would not, onwards and upwards we must go, if we would escape from our rocky prison. We took off our shoes and stowing them away in our pockets crept cautiously along the face of the cliff. The undertaking was perilous enough, the feeling of the sublime vanished in a moment, nor was I touched with one spark of the fire of romantic enterprise till I reached a safe platform three feet by six, and situated about midway between the ocean and the summit of the cliff. Here a huge slip of strata facilitated one's progress. The superincumbent rock had receded from the strata below, and this left a kind of natural road, though under any other circumstances we should have looked on it as a perilous path indeed. The dip of the strata was to the north at an angle of 40 degrees or thereabout, and such also was the level surface of our only possible pathway. But unencumbered by shoes we walked on easily, nay almost securely, resting our hands for support against the rocks above us.

Occasionally there intervened a mighty chasm in whose dark depths we could hear and often view the boiling surges. Over these in general we managed to spring, though once it was necessary to climb the overhanging rock at the real peril of our lives. We spent some time in examining the nests of some Herring Gulls, and then clambered on for another hundred yards to the corner of the rocks where a gio cuts into the land. Here we came to a dead stop, the cliff beyond was perpendicular as a castle wall. What was to be done? Return we could not, too many fearful chasms had been cleared on our progress hither to make us wish to retrace our steps, and indeed some I thought it would hardly be possible to pass from the side on which we now stood. I looked at the rock above, it was steep but apparently not very high and afforded some good footing, I called to Procter, up we went and after a few minutes' anxious scrambling, we stood in triumph upon the summit. Once more upon the level sward we directed our steps towards the Burgh of Cullswick, though we were separated from that interesting ruin by a sound or strait of half a mile in width. After making a rough sketch of the Burgh, we returned to dinner, and allow me to introduce you to the table of a Shetland landlord of the better kind.

Even at this season Mr Scott could furnish a repast worthy of a southern table. Fish in the summer is the most plentiful article of food, and today we had tusk, ling and cod, all fresh and admirably cooked, for a Shetland chef de cuisine piques himself not a little on the various modes of dressing the finny inhabitants of the ocean. Mutton, smoked beef and vegetables succeeded, and then to our surprise appeared a monstrous pudding, flanked by a bowl of thick, luscious cream that no hermit could resist. To this succeeded cheese, to that tea and toast, and an hour or two after came a copious supper, followed by sundry libations of brandy, rum, whisky or gin till at length we escaped to rest.

NOTES:

1   Second son of Francis Cholmeley of Brandsby, a year older than Charlton and his first cousin.

2   Presumably the Dr Cowie who appeared as the least craven of the Lerwick doctors in 1832.

3   The highest peak.

4   This passage by itself might suggest that Charlton and Cholmeley were the guilty parties, but they had no motive, and Charlton's description of the cradle in his journal of his 1852 visit contains no hint of an uneasy conscience.

5   'The mill stones are commonly formed of a micaceous gneiss, being from 30 to 36 inches in diameter. The flour or meal I can assert from personal experience to be freely mixed with micaceous and quartzose particles.' (E.C., Journal of June 15th)

6   'The name of Papa is derived from the Icelantic, and an inlet bearing that appellation yet exists in Iceland on the eastern coast of that country, close to the entrance to the Hammersfiord. Papa Litla or Papa Little as it is now termed was anciently a residence of the papas or Irish monks.' (E.C.)

7   Procter was evidently a tender hearted individual, for he 'used to moralise most piteously over the hard fate of his dear friends [as he called the birds], but always prudently abstained from giving utterance to his feelings till the poor bird lay dead upon his knee.' (E.C., Journal of June 18th)

8   His house was on the island of Vaila. Melby, which gave him his territorial title, is some miles to the north, directly opposite Papa Stour.

Shetland 1834

Foula and Papa Stour

MONDAY June 23rd. The dreadful howling of the storm this morning intimated to us too plainly we could not proceed to Foulah. A boat and crew of five men belonging to that island have been detained here since Friday last, and the poor fellows are sadly anxious to get home to their families. They have agreed to transport us to the island for twelve shillings, bag and baggage. The distance is eighteen miles across a stormy ocean: how a Deal boatsman would hold up his hands at the exorbitant fare.

As it would be impossible, even though the wind should abate, to venture upon the open sea before midnight, we resolved to visit the high hill of Sandness to the north and west of Vailley, and to examine the adjoining lakes for wild fowl. One of Mr Scott's men pulled us across from the island up to the head of the sound. Landing at a small harbour, near to which was the kirk and two dissenting chapels, we were met by Mr Kerr, the kind old Independent minister who had been our fellow-passenger on the *Magnus Troil*. After a short conversation we pushed on forward to the hill of Sandness, over bleak mossy moors, not perhaps so wet as those of the west of Northumberland but far exceeding them in barrenness. From the summit of the hill of Sandness, one of the highest in Shetland, the view was as extensive as any traveller could desire. To the south lies Foulah with its pointed mountains of sandstone, rising majestically to a height of nearly 2,000 feet from the Atlantic.[1] To the west lay almost at our feet Papa Stour, which from the commanding point on which we stood appeared low and flat, and its rocks of such varied and beauteous forms were too diminutive to be visible at this distance. To the east rose the swelling hills of Delting and Sandsting, where a long chain of lochs was all that varied the monotony of the barren scene. Northmavine with the bare granite summit of Roeness Hill bounded our prospect to the north, save where over the shoulder of the last named mountain rose a blue far distant hill, which was probably Saxafiord on Unst.

We descended the north side of the hill and directed our course towards the chain of lochs which lay in this direction between us and the sea. Near the first of these we fell in with some Whimbrels, the first we had seen in Shetland, but in vain did we seek for their nest or endeavour to procure a specimen of the bird; they were so shy that we concluded that they had not yet begun to breed. A little further on I discovered by my telescope a brace of wild duck sitting in a small creek on the opposite side of a large loch, and in an admirable situation for a shot. Cholmeley and I crossed round by the western extremity of the long piece of water, and we then crept up on our hands and knees till the ducks were nearly within reach, when to our disappointment Procter fired at a flapper on the opposite side of the lake. Away flew our game, and nought remained but to vent our spleen upon Procter, who however was too far away to hear distinctly our vituperations. We then sought in vain for some more wild ducks, and in the meantime Procter had wandered away to the eastward and I did not see him again till we met at Vailley. Cholmeley left me too to look for Procter, and I trudged off alone towards some inviting lochs to the northward. The hillside which I now descended was clothed with heather at least two feet high, and there can be no doubt that if the Red Grouse were once introduced they would thrive as well in Shetland as in the Orkneys. In a large loch, on the centre of which was an island, the Herring Gulls had established themselves in great numbers. A large brown hawk attracted my attention, it was probably an Osprey, and I cautiously followed it down to a narrow loch which communicated by a brook with the aforementioned large piece of water. This I crossed and creeping up the opposite bank I cautiously brought myself in view of the whole lake, when a Red-breasted Merganser flew out from the bank beneath me. As it passed at the distance of perhaps seventy yards I fired but the shot was too light to take effect, and a second barrel loaded with swan shot was discharged with no better success. To complete my discomfiture two other birds of the same species passed within a yard of my head as I was reloading my gun, and this was the climax of the misfortunes of the day. I waded with considerable peril to a small holm in the centre of the lake in the hopes of discovering there either the eggs or the young of the Merganser, but nothing was to be found and I returned wet and weary to the land. From thence I wandered still farther to the north towards a chain of lochs of great extent, but upon reaching the spot I found it consisted of one long tortuous piece of water, nowhere above thirty yards in breadth. To my sorrow not a bird was seen upon its surface, and I had unwittingly involved myself in its numerous windings from whence ere I could escape it cost me many a weary step. I heard now several shots from my companions to the south, I guessed them to be signals to join, but as the wind blew from that quarter it was impossible to answer them. How wild and desolate was this scene, not a tree, not a house, not a human being in sight, yet I loved it, I revelled in my solitude, I felt free as the birds around me, and I shouldered my gun and looked around me as proudly as did Crusoe in his desert island.

Another large loch lay before me, as I turned my back upon the sea and retraced my steps towards Vailley Sound. A large and perfect brough was situated in this loch, but the causeway of broad flat stones that led to it had disappeared beneath the water. I was told afterwards that some of the natives who are well acquainted with their submerged position still pass over by means of them to the brough, to obtain in the breeding season the eggs and young of the Herring Gull that have here taken refuge. The walls of the building are still at least 15 feet perpendicular above the level of the lake, but the interior, I am told, is a mass of ruins. I saw but little more as I returned over the mossy moors, and about 8 p.m. I came down pretty exactly on Vailley Sound, where Cholmeley and Procter had arrived about an hour before me.

It was about half past eleven when we retired to rest, the wind was due south, and the Foulah men expecting a change on the morrow talked of embarking at mid-day for their lonely isle. We therefore went late to rest, and wearied as we were, left much of our luggage to be packed up on the following morning.

Tuesday June 24th. At one this morning, having been scarce two hours in bed, we were roused by the Foulah men thundering at our door with the intelligence that the wind had changed and that they waited for us on the beach. We hurried on our clothes, packed up our luggage as well as time would permit and in a short half hour everything was stowed away in the boat. Mr Scott was already awake, and had prepared for us a large stock of sugar, tea and good oatmeal, none of which articles, said he, were to be found in Foulah, and in addition to all this he stowed away an entire bed with its accompanying sheets and blankets, which we should have sorely missed in that desert isle. We parted in sorrow from the kind hearted man whose benevolence has rendered him universally beloved, and whose house no one ever left without regret.

In Vailley Sound, bounded as it is by high hills on the West, all was smooth and quiet, and I observed with some surprise that Mr Scott at this early hour of the morning followed us along the shore to the farthest promontory of his island. But we soon saw good cause for his fears in the tremendous waves that we encountered upon entering the open Atlantic. As we rounded the point that projected on the western side of the Sound, the sea struck us all at once, so that one half of the boat seemed to be for an instant in smooth water, while the prow was lashed by the foaming waves. In a very short time the tossing of the waves had its usual effect upon Cholmeley, and even I felt for a few minutes giddy and somewhat squeamish, until the old medicine of a hard ship's biscuit revived me. Procter, of course, was as well as could be. He is an excellent sailor and for a landsman quite bold and venturesome upon the water.

The sea indeed was high enough to cause some anxiety among our boatmen, for the white, crested waves constantly discharged a portion of their summits into our boat, and soon rendered us as wet and uncomfortable as we could wish to be. The wind, which for some time had been a point or two to the east of south, now wore round to the westward, and blew right off the island of Foulah. All now wished to return to Vailley save the skipper Lawrence Ratter, one of the best seamen on the island, who thought that 'wi blessin' we might 'yet make him out'.

It was now three a.m. We made a long tack to the eastward, not without danger, as the seas curled right over our deeply laden boat. One of the crew, seated at the head of the boat, kept his eye upon the waves and warned the skipper of their near approach. Having run to the eastward for near an hour, we put about and bore up for Foulah, but alas, we soon found that we had lost way, instead of making any progress, by our last tack. Another consultation was held, but the skipper, though not adverse to returning, prevailed upon his crew to persevere, and these five men sate cheerfully down to their oars to pull a deeply laden boat against wind and tide for a distance of eight miles in a raging sea. For nearly three hours we made little or no progress, and just held our own, for the stacks of Foulah, the landmarks by which we were guided, remained in the same relative position to each other, and I almost despaired of reaching the island. At length, overpowered by the fatigues of the preceding day, I laid myself down to sleep on a wet sack, which contained our bedding and provisions.

On awaking almost powerless with the cold, I found to my great joy that we were within gunshot of the shore, and that I had enjoyed a good sound sleep of three hours, as it was now nine a.m. and we had left Vailley Sound at one in the morning. With a fair wind the voyage from Vailley to Foulah is often accomplished in three hours.

We landed at the inlet of Ham, the only harbour for boats on this iron bound coast, and so narrow is it that two boats cannot pass, or can hardly do so, on its waters. As soon as we touched the shore we were welcomed with great joy and cordiality by all the inhabitants, and in particular by the poor woman who kept the 'buith' or store close to the landing place. I soon found she had mistaken me for Mr Hewitson of Newcastle, who had visited the island two years before.

As soon as our luggage was landed some of our boat's crew, without staying to rest after such severe labour, set off up the cliffs to procure birds and their eggs, and in half an hour's time one fourth of the population of Foulah was hanging over the cliffs and adventuring their lives for a few pence. Their frail tenure of existence depended solely upon the support of a rope of hair or of bristles and hemp mixed together, which latter is by the rockmen considered much less liable to be cut by the sharp projecting stones than when the 'tow' is composed exclusively of either material.

We were ushered by the woman who had welcomed us into the only building on the island which could be dignified by the name of 'house'. By way of distinction it was named the 'buith' or, in Old Norse, the 'bude', because Mr Scott's factor, Mr Petersen, resided therein, and kept a small store of tobacco, spirits and fishing lines for the use of the inhabitants of Foulah. The house had formerly been constructed for Mr Scott of Vailley, the proprietor of the island, and it must have been to the inhabitants an architectural wonder, for it consisted of four stories and four rooms, two of which, at least, if not a third, had been painted and the ceilings whitewashed. The lower rooms were occupied by the woman and her family, who to our great joy never slept upstairs in the bedroom, of which we took possession.

We mounted to our abode with no small difficulty, for many of the stairs were broken or rotted away. On entering our chamber we rejoiced to observe that the roof was in most places entire, and that indeed was no small comfort in this rainy island. In a recess behind the door was a bedstead on which Mr Petersen slept when he was upon the island. We soon made up a comfortable peat fire and proceeded to dry our bedding, and Cholmeley, who was no doubt greatly exhausted by his sufferings during the voyage, lay down to rest on the bedstead, while Procter and I prepared a hearty breakfast. There was an old broken teapot in the house, and moreover exactly three teacups, so that we were able to enjoy the luxury of the China leaf. I may add that there was but one teaspoon in the house, and perhaps not another in the whole island. While the tea was 'maskin' the housekeeper brought upstairs a whole bicker of porridge, made with Foulah oatmeal, but this dish is always more savoury when the meal is coarse. Besides I must add in justice to the Foulah miller, that his meal smacks less of the grindstone than that I tasted in Shetland. There was an abundance of milk and two gloriously large horn spoons, with the aid of which Procter and I soon saw the bottom of the bicker.

Shortly after, whilst Procter was drying our soaked garments and Cholmeley was still resting on the bed, I left the house and proceeded on a survey of the island. I directed my steps towards the southern extremity, winding through a great many small patches of small corn, which appeared healthy enough, but like the grass around it was extremely short in the straws, and the potatoes did not look promising. Corn is however in a good year very abundant, but the crops are liable, when nearly ripe, to be shaken out and destroyed by the gales of the September Equinox. There are two or three fresh water lochs upon the island of no great extent, and their surface is at all times covered with great numbers of Herring Gulls, Kittiwakes etc. The island consists mainly of three large hills, Liorafield, Hamrifield and the Sneug, with a smaller eminence to the south called the Noup. Between this and the three former, there is a deep valley nearly on a level with the ocean, and running east and west, while the sides of the hills that bound it are extraordinarily steep without being absolutely perpendicular, and are covered to the very summit with short coarse herbage.

I passed a fresh water loch and the south eastern shoulder of Hamrifield, and was walking along the deep valley before mentioned when I was accosted by one of the natives. He said he had been over the rocks for birds, and wished particularly to know the species which I most wanted. I had taken care beforehand to make myself acquainted with the Foulah names for the different birds, to told him I wanted the Lyra (or Manx Puffin), the Tystie (Black Guillemot) and the Mootie (Stormy Petrel) along with Bonxies (Skua) and their eggs, and that I did not wish for either Longie, Tammy Nories, Brongies or Laarqukidins, in plain English for Guillemots, Puffins, Cormorants or Shags. Hearing this he drew forth a Lyra from beneath his jacket, and with it showed me its egg, a rarity indeed; he had taken it, he said, on the Noup about 50 yards below the top of the precipice. The birds are dreadfully savage, and bit his horny fingers most unmercifully.

I ordered the man to follow me, and retraced my steps with exaltation towards the 'buith', for Procter had utterly despaired of obtaining a single specimen of the Manx Puffin in Shetland. Right wondrously then was he rejoiced when I brought him the living bird and its egg. I found too on my return that some of the eggs of the Tystie and of Richardson Gull had already been offered for sale during my absence, and that for these he had given the extravagant sum of threepence each, and at this rate we should very soon have been ruined. Soon after a man came down from the hills with six eggs of the Skua Gull, and for these we did not object to give the sum just mentioned. However I told him, I did not wish any more of them, being anxious to preserve that noble bird from destruction. And now birds and eggs of all kinds poured in upon us, and we were constantly in treaty for more. The poor people were anxious enough for money, but received thankfully the small sums that we gave them for having risked their lives, and only in one instance did we meet with anything like discontent. One little boy brought me a quantity of the Cyprea Europea or common cowrie from the shore, and another, still more extraordinary merchandise, nothing less or more than a quantity of rounded quartz pebbles from the beach. But a penny made these little dealers perfectly happy. Fortunately I had brought with me from Lerwick a large assortment of Danish fourpenny, tenpenny and twopenny pieces. These I found to be of great use in Foulah, and indeed the coins of all nations appear to pass current in Shetland, for I received some French five franc pieces at the bank at Lerwick. A short time before we arrived a French smuggler had visited the west coast of Shetland and had landed some excellent Hollands in Foulah, of which we were able to procure as much as we wished for at eighteen pence a bottle.

Peat is luckily abundant in Foulah, and is dried and stacked with great dexterity and neatness by the inhabitants. Without this most necessary article, how comfortless would be their winter. But during that period there is occasionally another cause of high excitement, and of no inconsiderable profit to the Shetlander, in the shape of a wrecked vessel. It is a melancholy fact that the people of Foulah, along with those of the mainland, can never understand that a vessel cast on their iron bound coast does not by that very misfortune become their property. Before the time of Earl Patrick Stuart the Shetlanders are said to have been celebrated for their attention to mariners in distress, but this tyrant is said to have promulgated a law by which it was rendered penal for anyone to assist a shipwrecked mariner or to help them in any way towards the saving of their vessel. The original law, I suspect, cannot be found, and some strong circumstances have lately been brought forward to prove that the law of Earl Patrick Stuart was made with quite a different intention, namely to prevent the natives from plundering the wrecked vessels under pretence of rendering assistance. Be this as it may, the Shetlander, like the wrecker of Cornwall, is never sorry for a shipwreck, and it is always enumerated among his Godsends, with a boat's fare and a drove of whales. I could never make them comprehend the total immorality of these practices.

Another of their superstitions, obviously connected with this, is the repugnance they have to assisting a drowning man, under the idea that he will afterwards do them some deadly harm. Of this revolting belief a melancholy example occurred during the year 1834. A boat containing four men had left Quarff on the eastern coast of Shetland about six in the evening. While near Gulberwick a flann or blast of wind from the land upset the frail craft, and precipitated them all into the deep. At this time it was only dusk, and they were so near the land that their cries were distinctly heard. Not a single individual moved hand or foot to their relief. The people, all able bodied men, collected in a cottage near the beach, where they sat looking in each other's faces till the morning's dawn. Long ere that time the voices of the sufferers were hushed in the waves, but in the commencement of the night their cries for two hours broke upon the panic-struck group upon the shore, and were unheeded.

However it is to be hoped that few or none would now do what was perpetrated in the island of Yell many years ago. During a tremendous gale of wind a Dutch brig ran for shelter into the Bay of Houland, and casting anchor, attached herself for greater security by a strong cable to the rocks. During the night the cable was cut by the natives, the vessel totally wrecked, the crew drowned, and the spoils divided by the murderers.

One more tale of shipwreck, and I have done. In the month of April 1834 a vessel from Belfast, bound for Leith, was driven by a storm out of her course and struck during the night upon the western side of Foulah, at the foot of the rock called the Noup. The darkness prevented the wretched crew from judging of their situation. The mate and a young man named Robert Black jumped from the vessel when she struck upon the rocks, but the latter alone made good his footing. The unfortunate mate was crushed to pieces between the ship's hull and the shore, and in a few minutes the rest of the crew were swallowed up in the waves. For some time the poor lad remained on the ledge of rock upon which he had alighted, but despair aroused him to exertion, and he at length reached the top of the cliff. How he accomplished this in the dark, a height of at least two hundred feet perpendicular, it is impossible to say, but no Foulah man would attempt it in daylight and in his sober senses. It was just at the first morning's dawn of a cold wintry day that he gained the summit of the cliff, and reader may imagine his feelings as he gazed upon this most inhospitable-looking land. He descended into the deep valley between the Noup and Liorafield of which I have before spoken, and there by good fortune fell in with a man who at that early hour was returning from his peat stack with a load of fuel. The superstitious Foulah man was terrified by the apparition of a human figure advancing towards him all clothed in white, for the shipwrecked boy had nothing on but his shirt and trousers. His superstition warned him to flee, but ere he could escape, he was accosted by the sprite imploring his assistance and asking in piteous tone if he were in a Christian land. 'For' said my informant, 'he tought he might be mang cannibals.' 'Is it a trow² or a Christian man that speaks to me?' replied the cautious Shetlander. But ere he could well conclude his address, a hearty sailor-like grasp of the hand convinced him he was conversing with real flesh and blood. The poor lad was nursed with great care during his stay upon the island and left it full of gratitude to the hospitable natives.

In the evening after a meal on fish tusk and chickens we walked out to the fishermen's huts on the opposite side of the little islet of Ham. Of the numerous fishing lodges that I had entered in different parts of Shetland, none equalled these for comfort and convenience. The huts, which would barely hold six people, were partly sunk in the ground, I suppose to prevent their being overturned by the violence of the wind. In the centre, of course, was the fire, and around were arranged couches of green turf, soft and pleasant, whereon the tired fishermen reposed at night, and sate during the day when not employed at sea.

Their attention was greatly attracted by our double barrelled guns, which they had never before seen, and one man came actually from the other side of the island to see the guns which fired twice without reloading. A large circle of the islanders gathered around us in the immediate vicinity of the lodges, and just at the right moment a pigeon flew over our heads and was brought down in style by Cholmeley. It was the Rock Dove Columba Denas, and we wanted to preserve the specimen, but the man who picked it up instantly twisted off the head because, said he, 'You may then with safety eat the bird if you pull off the head and let him bleed well.' Had this any reference to the Jewish prohibition of eating blood? I assured them, however, in order to save my specimens for the future, that I had eaten many pigeons with the head on during my former visits, and had experienced no ill effects from such dangerous diet. But what pleased them most was the manner in which the bird was brought down upon the wing, for such as have guns upon the island never attempt anything beyond a sitting shot.

We then returned home to supper and after that prepared for bed. Cholmeley and I slept on the only couch, which we had brought from Mr Scott's, while poor Procter extended his length upon the floor, with some boat-cloaks and straw beneath. In the morning he said, however, that he had slept well, but added significantly rubbing himself, 'I think it was a little hard.' As soon as we had got to bed I expressed a hope that it would not rain in the night. 'Why?' asked Cholmeley. I did not speak but pointed to the bed top and to the clear blue sky that looked through many a rent in the roof. Fortunately no clouds obscured the blue expanse during the still night.

Wednesday June 25th. All this morning we were busily engaged in stuffing birds, cleaning guns, blowing eggs and the rest of the business of the travelling naturalist. The day was really warm, the thermometer at 12 noon stood at seventy in the shade, and the heat in our little low-roofed chamber was terribly oppressive. Looking through the one small window which lighted our apartment, I espied some pigeons feeding within gunshot of the door, I quietly took my gun, stole downstairs, astonished Procter with the report of a right and left shot close beneath him, and still more so when I brought him up a fine brace of pigeons for dinner. Today Mr Petersen the factor or steward of Mr Scott for Foulah came over from Vailley Sound; he assured me that Mr Scott had felt great alarm for our safety on the preceding morning.

During my stay in Foulah several people, hearing that I was a doctor, came to consult me about their various complaints. The chief disorders to which they seemed to be liable were skin diseases and affections of the chest, the former caused no doubt in a great measure by their fish diet and by the filth and dirt of their habitations, the latter, from the exposure to the sea in all weathers, and to the damp fogs of the Atlantic.

Among the instruments that I had brought with me to Shetland was a compound microscope which I exhibited one day to Lawrence Ratter and his crew. They looked through it and then burst into a fit of laughter, they examined every part of it again and again, at length Lawrence Ratter asked me 'if it was not one of those play acting things' that they had 'read about in books?' It was long ere I could convince him that there was no deception in the whole affair and that the insect, a flea, with which I can answer feelingly they were all well acquainted, was beneath the glasses and only increased in size by the operation. The camera lucida, the telescope, the klinometer and the rifle were all by turns most carefully examined, and excited their share of wonder.

Thursday June 26th. After remaining in the house to clean guns, skin birds and order the dinner we all marched out to ascend the summit of Liorafield and the Sneug. Our object in going there was chiefly to make war on the Skua Gulls, of which as yet we had obtained no specimens. This noble bird is now decreasing fast in numbers, Foulah and Roeness Hill in Shetland are the only British localities in which it breeds, and if not carefully protected it will soon be totally banished from there. Many fall a prey to the naturalist, but it is not in this way that the race will be exterminated. The Foulah men are themselves to blame, as they annually take without remorse the eggs of the noble bird from the heaths on which it breeds.

We wound round the southern shoulder of the mountain of Hamrifield, which rises 1,300 feet above the sea, and then turning towards the north, we ascended its steep sides and by the time I had reached the top I observed my companions far below engaged in the pursuit of some Richardson Gulls, Snipes etc., and quite forgetful of the noble game that awaited them above. Reclining at my ease on the smooth turf I watched for a while their ardour in the sport, but was soon aroused by a large bird wheeling and swooping just above my head. It was the Skua Gull, 'the Eagle of his tribe', and this was the very first time I had seen him. In my first surprise I fired hastily at him with buckshot, but nowise discomfited by so unceremonious a reception this magnificent bird continued to sail above me unharmed, as if to reconnoitre his enemy. I did not fire again, and was amply repaid for my forebearance by the pleasure of watching this noble gull in his native haunts. The flight of the Skua is extremely graceful, as is that of the whole of this genus, and their strength of wing is absolutely wonderful. They are much beloved by the inhabitants of Foulah, as they protect the lambs when feeding on the hills from the attacks of the Eagle. Whenever the tyrant of the air passes near their nests they attack him with the utmost fury, rising above him into the air, and then pouncing like a hawk upon his back with their beak and sharp crooked talons.

My companions toiled but slowly up the steep and grassy mountain and not wishing to await their coming up I moved on towards the summits of Liorafield and of the Sneug. The latter is the highest point in the island, rising 1,792 feet above the level of the sea. According to the late trigonometrical survey it is 50 feet higher than the summit of Roeness Hill in Northmavine, and is consequently the highest land in all the Shetland Archipelago. A small mop within a few yards of the summit of the hill forms the principal breeding place of the Skua Gull. Here from 10 to 20 pair of these noble birds were flying about, and as I approached three or four separated from the rest to drive off the intruder. On they came straight towards me, at the height of two or three yards above the ground. Not wishing, even for Natural History's sake, to endure any rough blows upon my head from their pinions I raised my gun when they were close to me, and

Edward Charlton as a young man.

From the journal of Edward Charlton

Lerwick.

Mill near Stenness.　　　　　　　　　　　　　　　　　*Edward Charlton*

Tingwall.　　　　　　　　　　　　　　　　　*Edward Charlton*

Holm of Noss.   *Edward Charlton*

Broch of Mousa.   *Edward Charlton*

Broch of Mousa.   *Edward Charlton*

Grind of the Navir.   *Edward Charlton*

Edward Charlton

Near Hillswick, road to Lerwick.

Roeness and Hillswick. *Edward Charlton*

though almost within reach of the barrel, these birds darted instantly upwards almost in a perpendicular direction to evade the threatened blow. On the preceding day they had attacked with the utmost fury the man who brought to us their eggs, and his head bore testimony to the violence of the blows they had received. After wheeling around me for some time one of the Skuas alighted at a short distance from me, and was very soon killed by a discharge of small shot, for I have never found shot of large size of any use for sea birds. Number five is good for almost everything. But this did not at all check the boldness of the rest, they still pounced on us the moment our eyes were averted from their movements. Procter and Cholmeley had now come up, and we remained long upon the summit of the highest hill in Shetland to contemplate the flight and habits of these rare and graceful birds.

We descended at length by the north side, which is excessively steep and much more rugged, and arrived at the buith to enjoy a true Shetland dinner. Some fresh tusk had been brought in this morning, and while the body of the fish was boiled the head was converted into 'ane crappit head', a savoury Shetland dish, prepared by stuffing that part with oatmeal, and then toasting it with abundance of butter before the fire. The liver too was chopped up into small pieces, and by a peculiar process dressed much to my taste, constituting another Shetland dish, the 'Livered Moggie'. Two fat chickens and a brace of pigeons were likewise soon demolished, and Mr Petersen brought out a bottle of Shetland Ale, clear as amber and sweet, though not with the heavy luscious flavour of the ale of Edinburgh. It was moreover very brisk so that we could almost believe it to have been seasoned with the tops of heather, as was done by the Pictish nations of old.

After dinner I walked out to visit Lawrence Ratter, who lived about a mile and a half from the buith. Calling at the house of one of his crew I was forced to partake of some milk and Hollands, and then proceeding on my way I was met at the door of his mansion by the skipper himself and conducted into the interior of his habitation. We entered, of course, in the true Norse fashion through the offices, or rather the 'outhouses', and from thence passed through one door after another to the chamber of dais, where I found seated his wife and children. Everything bore witness of a superior style to most of the cottages I had seen in Shetland. The whole wall was panelled in woodwork as clean as in Switzerland, and numerous cupboards of good workmanship were arranged around, and well filled to all appearances with good warm clothing of wadmead, and with carpenter's tools and fishing apparatus. It was indeed a remarkable fact to meet with so clean a house amidst the poor inhabitants of Foulah.

Satiated as I already was, the good woman forced me to partake of a bursten broonie with a huge bowl of rich thick milk. Lawrence Ratter informed me that an old man of the name of William Hendrie who lived in the adjoining 'toon' was the only individual yet remaining in Shetland who retained any remnants of Norse language which 100 years ago was almost universally prevalent in these islands. William Hendrie can still repeat the old ballad of the strife between the King of Norway and an Earl of Orkney on account of the marriage of the latter to his daughter in his absence and without his consent.

From the house of Lawrence Ratter at Gittorm we walked down to the sea, to view a magnificent perforated rock, the arch of which cannot be less than 100 feet in height, though still far inferior in size to that of Doreholm in Northmavine. Cholmeley here joined us, and Lawrence related to us a melancholy accident which occurred about two years before to his brother at this spot. He was stepping or rather springing from one rock to another to reach a large stack on which were the ruins of an ancient Brough now tenanted by sea gulls, when his foot slipped and he fell into the sea. As he rose a tremendous wave swept him from the rock and he disappeared for ever.

Leaving Ratter conversing with his crew as to the probability of our getting out of Foulah in the ensuing morning, I approached alone the brink of the precipice, when he loudly called me to keep off, as the banks frequently gave way beneath the slightest additional weight. Under his guidance we walked cautiously out upon a small promontory which commanded a view of the range of precipices, extending from the point where we stood to the Kaim, and facing us was an enormous wall, the whole western side of this island. The spot from which we viewed this magnificent scene was not more than 200 feet above the sea, but immediately beyond it rose the bank of Sorbarlie to the height of at least 900 feet perpendicular. At this measurement the cliffs continue to the Kaim, where the rock suddenly attains its utmost altitude and forms a sheer perpendicular precipice of 1,600 feet.

Lawrence Ratter pointed out to me several ledges a long way down the face of the cliff upon which he had been in search of eggs and birds, and what seemed odd enough to me at the time, he never calculated the entire height but only how low down he had descended from the summit. Many of his most daring feats had been accomplished on cliffs much lower than the Kaim. A year or two ago two ponies were playing on the top of Sorbarlie while Lawrence Ratter and his boat's crew were sailing past the cliff. One of them by accident rolled over the edge of the precipice. He fell at first perpendicularly but soon began to turn over, striking and rebounding from the face of the cliff till his shattered fragments arrived at the bottom. The boat rowed to the spot. The rocks around were bespattered with pieces of flesh, and a small portion of his lungs were all that could be found upon the water. True, the heavier portions of his carcase may have gone to the bottom.

But alas, it is not the brute creation alone that have met with destruction on these precipices. A considerable number of years ago a father and his two sons went to Kaim for the purpose of procuring eggs. The father being the more experienced went down first, and the sons followed according to seniority. In a short time the youngest son perceived the strands of the rope to be separating from the combined weight, and thinking it expedient that one life should be sacrificed to save two more, he whispered coolly to his brother beneath, 'Robie, cuit awa Da.' Poor Robie looked up, and saw in a moment the sad state of the case, but being endowed with more filial piety than his brother absolutely refused to disencumber the rope of his honoured parent. 'Dann,' quoth Magnus, 'I maa sney da tombe upon Robie and Da tooe.' It was no sooner said than done, and Magnus with a sorrowing heart regained the summit while the mangled corpses of Da and his dutiful Robie splashed into the Atlantic.

Another Foulahman was not, however, so happy as Magnus in getting rid of his relations. He and his wife were upon the same rope, and the gude wife was farthest down, when their thread of life showed evident signs of holding out no longer. Without delay he sacrificed his rib away, she flew whirling and screaming like a wounded sea gull, and her husband returned home to mourn for his departed spouse. Great indeed was his affliction and as usual the neighbours had assembled to offer all the consolation in their power, when the door burst open and in rushed the gude wife herself, dripping from the salt sea, and giving convincing proof by means of her fists and tongue that she was no disembodied sprite, but true flesh and blood. How matters were made up with her now perhaps still more disconsolate husband, history does not inform us, but she escaped from supposed certain destruction by the wind having caught her petticoats in the descent, and thus held her supported by a parachute, till she sank gracefully into ocean's bosom, where by good chance a passing boat picked her up.

Friday June 27th. To hold our additional luggage, which had so much increased in bulk during our sojourn on the island, I purchased this morning a straw basket or capie which answered all our purposes. We took leave of Mr Petersen who is at once factor, schoolmaster and parson, and getting into our boat we sailed away with a fair wind for Papa Stour. As we neared the island its rocks rose majestically out of the blue sea, and though the island is no great height, its cliffs are cut out and shaped with the most fantastic forms. The sound between Papa and the Mainland is at all times a dangerous passage, but to us and our boatmen it was particularly so from the fact of only one being acquainted with its hidden rocks and furious currents. The day was bright and sunny, the wind fair, and long, heavy waves dashed on the western shore of Papa and on the two Ve Skerries still further out in the Atlantic, while in the Sound itself all was tranquil, and we glided safely and securely to the little harbour on the east side of the island. We landed in all haste about two p.m., having accomplished the eighteen miles from Foulah in something less than three hours.

Our boatmen were anxious to avail themselves of the fair wind to return to their much loved island, and having carried our luggage up to the 'Ha' House', the residence of Mr Gideon Henderson, they left us, and we soon saw their sails careering through the Sound on their homeward voyage. The Ha' House of Papa Stour was a large edifice strongly built in the plainest style, and roofed with heavy grey slate. It is the only building of any consideration in the island, the rest are wretched hovels, and worse here than in any other part of Shetland. Mr Henderson had crossed over to the mainland, but we were most hospitably received by his sisters, and in the evening he himself returned to give us a hearty welcome to his sea-girt domain. Here we also met the Hon Mr Lindsay Balcarres, about whom so much has been written and declaimed, and on whose account Gideon Henderson has been so illiberally abused. It would be here out of place to enter upon the merits of the case. My own opinion, founded upon actual acquaintance with all the parties, is that Mr Henderson is a deeply injured man, that the Hon. Lindsay Balcarres is a most dangerous lunatic, and that Miss Weston, who was the cause of all the mischief, is not a whit more sane than the man in whose behalf she excited herself so much.

After dinner I walked round the island with Mr Henderson, and about 9 p.m. I was sent for in great haste to bleed a man who had just fallen down in a fit. I bled him, but was soon afterwards sorry that I had done so, as I discovered him to be labouring under symptoms of influenza, which at that time was very prevalent in the West of Shetland. Two of Mr Henderson's children were now attacked by the same disease. As I was returning from the cottage I began myself to feel very unwell, and from that hour I may date the commencement of the illness which so effectually put an end to all my enterprises in Shetland.

Saturday June 28th. The herring season was now at its height and some magnificent fish of that species taken from the sea but half an hour before graced the breakfast table of Mr Henderson. The day was beautiful and our kind host had a boat in waiting for us on the beach to convey us to the rocks on the western side of Papa. Mr Nichol in Edinburgh had assured me that the rocks of Papa were by far the most extraordinary that he had met with in Shetland, and with this opinion I fully coincide.

As soon as we had stepped into the boat Mr Henderson gave the signal to his three stout boatmen and we glided out of the little cove towards the rocks on its eastern side. Here we entered suddenly a vast cave or 'helyer' through which the sea at all times flowed. For a few minutes we were enveloped in darkness, and then on a sudden a bright luminous ray broke upon us from a perforation in the rock and revealed the variegated coralline and tangled seaweed which clothed the rocky bottom a fathom or two beneath our boat. To the right and left branched off various helyers, some totally dark, others partially illuminated at some distances from above but too narrow for our boat to enter. No wonder that the Papa men are considered to be the most superstitious of all the Shetlanders, for who could traverse these marine abodes without a hope of coming at every turn upon some merman old and grey?[3]

Sunday June 29th. This day was nearly all spent in bed, but in the afternoon I was able to sit up. Cholmeley and Procter went in the morning to the Methodist Meeting House, for even in this distant land have these zealous men extended their labours. My companions reported the Meeting House to be one of the rudest edifices on the island, and to their dismay, on entering it not a seat of any kind was to be seen. But this in no wise troubled the zealous congregation, who seemed to take it as matter of course that they must provide accommodation for themselves. Around the door were scattered abundance of large stones, and much were the visitors astonished when every man, woman and child as they came in, lifted a stone of the size proportioned to their strength and forthwith carried it into the house of prayer. Their behaviour during divine service was quiet and orderly, and at the conclusion each in like manner lifted the stone they had sat upon and carried it beyond the door of the Meeting House. Not content with once a day church, Cholmeley and Procter went in the evening to the Sunday School, but the singing then they said was execrable, and the church bitterly cold, as most of the windows were destitute of glass.

Monday June 30th. During the whole of this day the rain fell heavily, and had it been the finest weather possible I was too weak and ill to venture out. Here in this distant land no medicines were to be procured, nor could medical assistance easily be obtained, even if, when got, it was of any worth from the rude followers of Aesculapius in Shetland. We therefore packed up all our luggage, which had now grown to an overwhelming bulk, and resolved should the wind be fair to start for Ollaberry in Northmavine on the morrow.

Thursday July 1st. After breakfast we engaged a boat with four men to convey us to Ollaberry, but at the time we left Papa we were undecided as to whether we should draw the boat over the Gluss of Air,[1] or take the longer circuit through shorter overland journey by Mavis Grind. Mr Henderson and his ward Lindsay accompanied us to the boat, and the latter, as we were forewarned, showed no small anxiety to accompany us. Passing Frowken Stack on the left, we bore right away for the Gluss of Air, discussing as we sailed along the state of the tides and the opposing currents we should meet with on our progress. The day was warm and fine, the sea too was smooth which is but rarely the case in the stormy bay of St Magnus. Our old skipper, a Papa man of most lugubrious aspect, entertained us as he sat at the helm with a dismal history of a ferocious giant who formerly inhabited the island of Vementry. He solemnly assured me that he had seen the cave where the monster dwelt, and had there handled the bones of the sheep and oxen wherewith he had filled his rapacious maw. I did not doubt that he had seen some bones in a cave upon that island, but was as little disposed to refer them to the giant, as their presence could easily be otherwise accounted for. Sheep stealing was in former times but too common in Shetland, and in the ancient records of the country there exist many savage enactments against this crime.

By the rest of Shetland the Papa men are regarded as ignorant savages, and they in turn look down with pity upon the poor natives of Foulah, and they again commiserate the lot of the inhabitants of Fair Isle. Indeed, I cannot say that I found the Papa men very intelligent, and they are by far the most superstitious of all the Shetlanders. Our helmsman was a firm believer in trows, fairies and all sorts of witchcraft. I asked him if he himself had ever been favoured with a view of these supernatural beings. He answered that this had but once occurred to him during his life. In returning one Sunday from the Kirk at Hillswick, he was surprised to observe a man who without speaking a word walked over the hill close by him and accompanied him in silence for a considerable distance. 'But,' said I, 'this might have been a mere man of flesh and blood, and his behaviour was by no means supernatural.' 'Ah,' said he, 'but we went round a little knowe, and when I came to da order seide, da man was gan. Dat was a trow.' And nothing could persuade him to the contrary.

We had now a fair wind which carried us through St Magnus Bay at a fair rate, till we found ourselves under the lee of the island of Muckle Roe. From the boat I could at a distance see the junction of the granite and greenstone rocks, to investigate which had been one of my chief objects in coming to Shetland, but I was today too ill to land, and had we done so we should not have reached Ollaberry that night. As the tide was very low, and our luggage heavy, we resolved to go round by Mavis Grind, instead of taking the longer, and consequently more laborious portage over the Air. Here we unloaded the boat, and having first carried over our luggage, the craft itself was dragged by our united exertions across the narrow isthmus, not more in this spot than one hundred yards in breadth, which connects Northmavine with the Mainland. Reloading our boat we pushed on without further delay or adventure to Ollaberry and arrived there about five in the afternoon. To our disappointment Mr Cheyne was not at home, but this was by no means so serious a consideration as it would have been in more southern climes.

We of course took possession of the house, and I felt as if I had already regained my health. But Cholmeley now complained a little, so I made him keep in bed and, what was worst of all, I put him upon low diet.

NOTES:

1   Charlton overstates the altitudes on Foula.

2   A Shetland troll; see below, journal of July 1st.

3   Besides exploring the caves of Papa in search of seals and Eider duck the party rowed past the Horn of Papa to the Lyra and Fugle Skerries.

4   Perhaps because he was suffering from fever Charlton seems to have confused names here. By 'Gluss of Air' he can hardly mean Gluss Ayre, since that is not a portage alternative to Mavis Grind; the isthmus at Brae, however, is an alternative, and Charlton may be referring to that.

Shetland 1834

Sickness and Return

[Charlton's sickness kept him indoors for three days, but on July 5th he felt sufficiently convalescent to ride Mr Cheyne's pony over to geologise at Collafirth and on the 7th accompanied Cholmeley and Procter by boat as far as Feideland (Fethaland). This, however, was only a temporary remission, and in the end all three were incapacitated.]

MONDAY July 7th. We set off this morning at an early hour to Feideland where we were certain of most ample employment for our hammers. The weather was warm, and a light air playing on the face of the waters carried us rapidly towards the wished for spot.

Feideland was formerly the largest fishing station in Shetland, but it has now greatly diminished in importance. In former times seventy or eighty six-oared boats rowed from hence to the Haaf; this year there were but 22 and a still further reduction of this number is anticipated. The fish have certainly become more scarce upon the coast, and the bad weather that has prevailed during the last three summers has prevented the fishermen from visiting their most productive and abundant haunts. I know of few scenes more wild and desolate than that on the west coast of the Feideland. The Ramney Stacks, rocks almost inaccessible to man, the rugged back of Roeness Hill and the wild Atlantic surges beating on this iron bound coast all impress the mind with a feeling of awe and give a savage character to the landscape that cannot be described.

The Klebert Gio, like that in Fetlar of the same name, is so called from the abundance of steatite which it contains, and there also we found veins and beds of beautiful asbestos, green chlorite, hornblende and anthophyllite. On a slanting rock on its southern side, before descending into the gio, is an inscription in rude characters which then did not much interest me, but which I now bitterly regret that I did not accurately copy. It was undoubtedly runic, the letters were graven deep in the anthophyllite rock, in some parts they were as deep as three inches into the stony face of the cliff.

Returning to the fishing boats I was invited into the berth by Magnus Tulloch, one who had come with us from Ollaberry, and was therein regaled with a whisky bland and biscuit in as original a manner as ever traveller dined in a wilderness. One half of this house was filled with salt, and his hammock hung directly above the store of this wholesome condiment! Hear, and attend, ye lovers of salt fish! A board served for a desk, a cask of whisky was his chair, and other furniture there was none, in this the richest mansion in Feideland.

By the time we re-entered the boat the rain had begun to fall, and the wind became adverse. On rounding the southernmost point at the entrance of the harbour we were met by a severe and cutting blast, which made us shiver in our boat-cloaks as our dress was already damped by the rain. As we returned along by the coast we rowed into a small cave, in which we had observed the nests of several Green Cormorants. One of these birds we wounded by a shot, and as he appeared very unwilling to dive, we hemmed him towards the extremity of the cave. At the moment when we thought ourselves secure of the prize, he disappeared beneath the boat, and as we did not see him rise again we concluded that he had sunk to the bottom, and there died while holding fast by the seaweed and tangles. A little further on we shot an Oyster-Catcher, upon which one of our boatmen declared that we should have a foul wind all the way home, for having slain so good a bird, which by the people of Northmavine is regarded as sacred. This time he was right, and it was four hours before we reached Ollaberry. We sat all this time exposed to a cold driving rain which to me was anything but agreeable, and in the sequel proved most disastrous to our expedition. It was late ere we reached Ollaberry wet and weary, and though we retired soon to bed it was not to rest, for I passed a feverish night.

Tuesday July 8th. Today I felt so unwell that I gave up all hopes of escaping an attack of fever. In the evening Cholmeley and Procter went off to Apeter, while I remained at Ollaberry, and on the following Friday was obliged to take to my bed. On the next day Cholmeley returned from Apeter in no better plight then myself, having been dreadfully fatigued on the previous day by a long walk round the west coast of Northmavine from Hillswick to Hamnavoe in a storm of wind and rain. We were thus both fairly laid up, and we did not leave our beds till the Saturday following,[1] when no trace of fever remained.

During my illness I wished to be bled, and accordingly a true barber chirurgeon made his appearance. He was by trade a fisherman, and nowise distinguished from the rest of his occupation save that he had learned the mysterious art of cutting hair and phlebotomy. On the previous day he had shorn my head of its fair covering, and at 'elka lock he shredd' he stayed his hand and exclaimed 'Alas! Alas! To cuit sic bonny hair, but on da saiy aye dat soft hair has hard heart.' I hoped that such was not my case. When, however, the following morning I sent for him to bleed, he at first resolutely refused, on the singular pleas that he had never bled a gentleman in his whole life.

On the kindness of Mr Cheyne during this sad period it is needless and impossible to speak, those only who have partaken of his hospitable table can appreciate this. It may seem strange to many that we should thus travel from house to house, without even a recommendation, but in these remote countries the appearance of a stranger is hailed as a godsend by the landholders, as well as by the very intelligent natives in their humble peasants' dwellings. I have often been astonished as well as amused at the acuteness of the remarks made by the common people upon the actions and sayings of more refined society which they had read of in the newspapers.

During this long and tedious time Procter was busily engaged in procuring specimens of Natural History, and I sent him for that purpose into different parts of Northmavine, where he obtained several of the Whimbrel, the Red-throated Diver, and of Richardson's and the Skua Gulls. At length in climbing over a high stone wall, a heavy stone fell upon and injured him so severely that he was forced to take to his bed about the time that we were able to move again about the house. The stone walls of Shetland are indeed unsafe to clamber over, being frequently carried up to the height of 6 or 8 feet with a single breadth of stone. This last accident was the climax of our misfortunes.

NOTE:

1   Presumably July 24th; but the journal has a gap at about this time, and the dates when they resume do not tally.

Shetland 1834

Chasing the *Magnus Troil*

MONDAY 26th July. It was on this morning that I threw open the front door of the house at Ollaberry and sallied forth wrapped in my best cloak to enjoy one of the warmest and finest days I had ever experienced in Shetland. I felt indeed a thrill of freedom, after having been shut up fifteen days in a low room with one small window that looked out on the sky.

I this day received a letter from Mr Yorston of Lerwick concerning the *Magnus Troil,* whose arrival at Ollaberry I had anxiously expected today. However the vessel did not appear, nor could I learn that she had been seen going into Taphs [Tofts] Voe to call at Mossbank. The season for birds had now nearly passed, and as it would be long ere I could recommence my labours with the hammer, I relinquished my intention of revisiting the North Isles of Shetland, and determined upon an immediate return to Edinburgh by the *Magnus Troil.*

Tuesday July 27th. Having heard nothing of the *Magnus Troil,* we determined on an express to Taphs Voe to enquire for that vessel. As we feared that she would give us but short notice of her departure we packed up our most bulky luggage and kept ourselves in readiness to start. Arthur Smith brought over to us a pair of tuskars (instruments used for cutting peat, and which we wished to take with us to the South). As we did not exactly understand the way of using them, we dragged our weakened frames with great difficulty about three hundred yards up the hill above Ollaberry, that Arthur Sanderson might there show us the method of casting the peats. It was no great labour, but as I redescended the hill I felt that I had done enough for the day, and looked forward to a good night's sleep to recruit me for the morrow.

But that night's rest I was not destined to enjoy. On reaching the house we perceived our express returning through Yell Sound. We awaited it anxiously on the shore, and heard to our utter dismay that the *Magnus Troil* had been in Taphs Voe last night, and after remaining there for an hour or two, had proceeded straight to Lerwick, from whence at two o'clock this day she was to start for Leith. What was to be done? It was but a day or two since we had risen from a bed of sickness, and this was but the second morning that we had ventured into the open air; and yet if we had hoped to come up with the vessel we must run the risk of being out all night at sea in an open boat. We deliberated for a moment and then determined to reach Lerwick that evening if possible, though it was then three p.m., and another hour must elapse before everything could be got ready for our voyage. It is seldom that a Shetland vessel sails on the appointed day, so I thought we had a good chance of finding the *Magnus* in harbour on our arrival at Lerwick. The evening promised well, and if the breeze which had been blowing all day still held up, we calculated upon reaching Lerwick by about 11 p.m., which at this season of the year could be only about nightfall in the northern regions.

In an hour our boat was ready at the pier, our luggage was on board and with light hearts we took leave of all Mr Cheyne's dependants, not doubting of reaching our destination that night. But old Peter, an ancient mariner, shook his head and feared, he said, that the wind would not hold, as he saw the mist settling down on the opposite coast of Yell. And there, sure enough, were the dark grey clouds, rolling down the black hills and creeping like an advancing tide across the ocean.

The tide was full against us as we left Ollaberry, and we hoped earnestly for a strong and steady breeze to enable us to encounter the fearful currents in Yell Sound, which have always been an object of terror to the Shetland mariner. About six p.m. we entered the Sound, keeping close in shore along the edge of the tide, which ran boiling along the centre of the narrow strait, while on either side the water was still and smooth as glass. The wind, which for the last half hour had been light and shifting, now veered round the north east, and joined with the current in opposing our progress. Still we consoled ourselves with the thought that we always gained a little way as we tacked from one side to the other of the narrow Sound. At sunset a thick mist fell upon us just before we reached the mouth of Taphs Voe, and as it closed around had a most singular and ominous appearance. The sun, just sinking behind the Ness of Ollaberry, still cheered us in some degree with his light, for the fog, though impenetrable on all other sides, formed in the west a low, deep archway, through which the sunbeams streamed upon the water almost up to our boat. It seemed as though we had entered some vast cavern, and were about to explore its hidden recesses, while the daylight became fainter and more uncertain as we advanced further from its mouth.

At ten p.m. it fell dead calm, and a heavy, warm mist enveloped the boat and rendered everything therein wet and uncomfortable. However we were well provided against the weather, having carried off several blankets from Ollaberry. During the two succeeding hours we made little more than three miles, and then, on partial dispersion of the fog, we discovered that we were now abreast of Mossbank. A council was now held, yet like the ancient Persians[1] we first addressed ourselves to the brandy bottle and leg of mutton. Supper ended, we by no means felt inclined to pass the night upon the same spot, which indeed it was now possible we should do, unless a speedy change in our favour in the shape of a good strong westerly breeze should spring up to carry us round the Ness of Lunna. It now wanted but half an hour of midnight, the tide, though running in our favour, would avail us but little in this heavy boat, and it was the unanimous opinion that it would be impossible to reach round Lunna Ness ere the stream should again be setting to the west. Lunna Ness is a long and narrow promontory, running out into the sea from the north east part of the mainland, and round this headland the tide rushes with tremendous power.

In the obscurity of the night we therefore determined to run in for the Banks of Lunna where the Ness, which is five or six miles in length, is joined by a low isthmus two or three hundred yards broad to the mainland. Guided by the compass we hoped to make this point in about an hour, and there to obtain a boat which from the other side would speedily convey us to Lerwick. The helm was therefore put about, and our course, from being nearly east by north, was altered to south south west. After a short pull we again tacked to the east as the boatmen seemed to doubt a little about the latitude they had got into, and from time to time we lay to and rested upon our oars, to listen for the barking of a dog or the restless dash of waves upon this iron coast. The thick mist gave rise to many a mistake, and the cry of land was given in whatever quarter we turned our prow.

Twelve o'clock had passed when a huge dark object seemed to move along the water towards our boat, and the experienced eyes of our steersman soon pronounced it to be the wished for shore. Though the sea was calm and smooth as glass we kept well out into the open water lest we might encounter some of the baas or sunken rocks which are the terror the Shetland mariner. We kept along in this way for a considerable time. Suddenly the man in the bow called out 'A baa! A baa!', and to our utter consternation the black head of a sunk rock appeared not above two feet in front of us, at times uncovered, and then again sinking deceitfully beneath the surface. By one vigorous stroke of the oar we happily escaped the threatened danger, but had the baa broke under us in the awful manner I have once experienced, some of us, I fear, would hardly have had strength or skill to reach the shore.

The crew now candidly confessed that they did not know where they were, and it was agreed that we should return about half a mile to where we had heard the barking of a dog, and then engage a pilot to the Banks of Lunna. With great difficulty we ran the boat against some low rocks on the shore, and one of the crew, stripping off his shoes and stockings, waded out in quest of the habitations of man. The barking of a dog was again heard, and directed by the sound he pursued his way and was soon lost to us in the mist. Through the silence of the night, however, we plainly heard his footsteps, and at length heard him knock at a door, while at the same time he was saluted by the yells of at least a score of dogs, which indicated that the town was of no inconsiderable size. After a long parley he brought down with him an old man as a pilot, who however was by no means the most active of his profession. He was lame of one leg and nearly blind of both his eyes. But this was a case of emergency, and in so thick a mist the best of eyes would have been of no great service.

For a time we made good progress, the old man took the helm, and munched biscuit and gabbered away about our probability of finding a boat at the Banks of Lunna. At length land was espied, but in the opposite quarter to that on which we had expected to meet with the shore. Our old pilot soon perceived his mistake (we had got too clear of the west side of the narrow voe), and he afterwards attended more carefully to the indications of the compass. At half past one a.m. the fog partially cleared and we saw above the stars, while to the east there appeared 'the first grey tints of coming dawn'. Passing a few small islands we entered a little bay, and soon found ourselves in the midst of what might be called a populous neighbourhood.

We sprang joyfully on the beach, and leaving the rest to unload our luggage, walked across with one of the crew to the other side of the neck of land. Great was our disappointment when we found that no boat was lying there in a state fit to go to sea. A large barge lay on the sand, but it was guiltless of paint, and through its shattered side gaped many a hideous rent. Beside it in equally wretched condition were two or three old whillys. Nearer to the spot where we had landed lay a fine six-oared boat, but that very day it had been tarred within and without, so that even had we ventured ourselves in it, we should never have left it again at Lerwick.

Three o'clock came, and we were still standing undecided on the beach. Return we would not. Even though the vessel had already sailed for Leith, we knew we could easily revisit the North Isles by means of the packet, or should the long exposure to the damp night air cause a return of the fever, we should at least at Lerwick have the best medical advice and attendance that Shetland could afford. At length it was decided that two men should be dispatched over the hills to the place where we had obtained our old pilot, as we were told that there a six-oared boat was to be procured with an efficient crew. The boat, however, would have to round the Ness of Lunna in order to take us up on the other side, and from the great extent of the promontory it would be past six a.m. ere they could reach us on the eastern shore.

For nearly an hour after the departure of our messenger I remained standing by the luggage on the beach. The sun had now risen, but though clear and warm overhead, a grey mist still hung over the water. We endeavoured to procure some tea, but the owner of the 'buith' had gone to Lerwick and taken the key of the store along with him. About half past four a man came down from a cottage at some distance and begged me to go up there and rest myself until the boat should arrive. I availed myself of this kind invitation and another man offered to be my guide thither. In the meantime my new host pushed off in his boat to procure the morning's meal for his family, and he and his craft soon disappeared in the mist. I heard the splash of his oars and his blithe song long after he was hidden from my sight, and once when the fog cleared for a few minutes I could see his small bark lying motionless on the glassy surface of the bay. On arriving at the cottage we obtained admittance after some loud knocking had roused the inhabitants. They did not, however, express any surprise at being thus intruded upon by strangers at this unseasonable hour, and this could only arise from the true Shetland spirit of hospitality, where the wayside traveller is looked upon as honouring the dwelling in which he seeks repose. We were accommodated with chairs, a rare article of furniture in a Shetland dwelling house, but it was in vain that we endeavoured to sleep. When the door was closed the smoke arose from the fire in the centre and nearly took away our breath, while at the same time it pained our eyes so sharply that we rushed in despair to the door and threw it wide open again as before. And then the sea breeze blew around us so cold and freezing that our invalid forms shivered in the blast. And to add to our discomfort Procter now fell asleep, and by his loud nasal tones effectually drove away all prospects of repose. As rest was out of the question I betook myself to eating, and thus the minutes flew quickly by till we rose to depart at seven a.m.

At the door we met the host returning from his fishing excursion with a most ample supply of codlings and haddocks, and on arriving at the shore we found a capital craft with six of the stoutest looking boatmen I had ever seen in Shetland. The men of Lunna pride themselves much on their rowing, nor were they this time wanting to their ancient fame, for the boat literally flew through the water under the influence of their vigorous arms. The hot sun overhead had not, however, cleared away the mist, and we were obliged to guide ourselves by the compass. I was half tempted to smile at the small compass the steersman held upon his knee when the old man said 'True lamm, dat is small, but he has stuid by me in da day of need. Wid him I sailed from da banks o Norroway til da Fair Isle in da grit storm.' 'Your name, then,' I said, 'is John Irving?' 'Ya, dat's what it is in truth lamm.'

I was not mistaken, this was the old man who was out in the great storm of 1832 from the Monday to the Saturday night, and for the last two days there was no food in the boat.[2] It was he who had kept up the sinking spirits of his crew, who several times were tempted to lie down in the bottom of the boat and abandon themselves to the mercy of those elements which seemed leagued against them for their destruction. I asked if he saw any other boats go down near him. 'Oh lamm, I saw two goodly sones of my ain bluid sink in da water by my side, but the Lord was pleased to spare the old father to be a help til his family. On da Tuesday night we saw not a single sail and we fand no sight of da land til da Friday at sundown. Dat was da Fair Isle, and we toyght it was da Noup od Noss, and da wind it blew aff da land, and we should have set foot na mair upon da shore, if da guid men had na comed aff from da Fair Isle in a peerie boat to pull us to da Isle, for lamm, a fasting man can do but little work.'

Our crew, however, had evidently broken their fast. They pulled so well that in a short time we had passed the Island of Whalsey, and the really splendid mansion of Mr Bruce of Symbister, which however is built in a situation which exposes it equally to all the winds of Heaven. It was now twelve o'clock and we calculated on reaching Lerwick in an hour. The mist thickened about us, and it was only at long intervals that we obtained a view of the coast to direct us on our voyage. At one p.m. I heard the cries of sea birds and perceived that the water changed its colour, and in a few minutes the conglomerate rocks of Rovie Head were close upon our starboard bow. We were therefore now at the entrance of the harbour of Bressay Sound, and we could already distinguish the masts of ships lying off the town of Lerwick. Every eye was now strained to catch a glimpse of the *Magnus Troil*. It was a moment of anxious suspense, but at length by means of the telescope I made out the broad arrows at the mast heads, and joyfully assured my companions that the wished for vessel was still in the harbour.

We were pulled to Peter Williamson's to take up the rest of our luggage and to recruit our strength with a hearty breakfast. Here we met Mr Cheyne, and William Cameron,[3] the latter for the first time during the expedition. Leaving Procter to pack up, we took boat and went across water to Gardie[4]. Dinner was announced there at four p.m. as the ship was to sail at six. And then were set before us something more than the usual dainties of Hialtaland: melons and grapes graced the board, and both were the produce of a Shetland garden. As we were chatting over our wine, the colours of the

Magnus Troil floated out at the foremast head. We took a hurried leave of our kind entertainers and recrossed the Sound to Lerwick to see that all our luggage was removed from our former lodging. Procter had filled six large boxes with the spoils of the Shetland Archipelago, and these we rapidly conveyed on board about seven p.m., when the vessel moved out of the harbour with a very moderate wind.

[This was the evening of Wednesday July 29th; the *Magnus Troil* reached Leith at six p.m. on Saturday August 1st.]

NOTES:

1   Who, according to Herodotus I.133.4, deliberated twice, once drunk and once sober.
2   See pages 17-18 above.
3   Charlton's host on Unst in 1832.
4   Home of Mr and Mrs Mouat on the island of Bressay.

Shetland 1852

Introduction

NEARLY twenty years had elapsed since I had visited the remote Shetland Islands, and during that period I had traversed a large portion of Europe, and had subsequently settled down to the practice of my profession at Newcastle. For 14 summers, with the exception of a brief visit in 1851 to the Great Exhibition, I had enjoyed no holiday, or at all events had not ventured above 100 miles from the town where I lived; but the old spirit of travelling, though it had thus been kept down, was not extinguished, and it now revived, with the additional plea of the necessity of relaxation after so long a period of assiduous exertion.

I determined, then, to allow myself a fortnight's excursion, but at the very beginning I found myself in the pleasing dilemma of having to choose the location for my temporary repose. The Continent of Europe was too distant, at least the lakes and mountains and glorious scenery of Switzerland were not yet united by railway to Belgium or to France, and Paris or Brussels would be but exchanging the bustle of one large town for the still greater turmoil of a metropolis. I longed, too, for an extended sea voyage, for I had ever retained my early predilections for the blue sea, and thus my mind reverted to the Northern Isles, with their wild scenery, their rich stores of natural history, and the perfect liberty and freedom from control in a land where no game laws, no fear of action for trespass, could come in the way to mar the pleasure of an excursion. There were, too, old recollections connected with these isles, old friends and familiar faces were yet to be found there, and old localities to be revisited where I had enjoyed many happy days. I was curious also to learn how the communication was now kept up between Shetland and the mainland, and what improvements if any had been effected in the last 20 years in these distant isles.

In Mr George Caley I was so fortunate as to meet with a suitable companion, congenial in every respect and possessed of that happy spirit which laughs at all toil and accommodates itself to every variety of circumstances. Caley had never penetrated further into Scotland than Loch Lomond, and my descriptions of Shetland fairly enlisted him for the journey. By a fortunate coincidence I was enabled to make arrangements with my professional bretheren to attend to my practice during my absence, and having thus disposed of the last source of anxiety, on Thursday morning, July 1st, I started at 6 a.m. by railway to Edinburgh to spend the afternoon there in the society of Dr Daniel Wilson, the Secretary of the Society of Antiquaries, while Caley was to sail by the *Britannia* at 3 p.m. and join me at Granton Pier the next morning.

July 2nd. At half past seven this morning I found Caley in the coffee room of the Black Bull in Leith Street where I had slept. He had arrived at Leith at 2 a.m. by the *Britannia* steamer, after a most favourable passage from Newcastle of only nine hours and a half. We set off directly after breakfast by the omnibus for Granton pier, where we arrived in a tremendous shower of rain. I had had too much experience in travelling to believe that the boat would start at the time appointed, but to my surprise all was ready at half past nine, and clearing the shelter of the pier we were soon exposed to the wind, which drove down the rain with additional fury upon our heads.

[The ship, the SS *Queen*, Captain Campbell, put in at Aberdeen, Wick and Kirkwall, reaching Lerwick on Sunday July 4th. Charlton has a lively description of the fishwives of Wick.]

July 3rd. The herring season had just commenced, the produce of the previous night's fishing had been brought on shore, and hundreds of women were actively engaged in preparing the fish for the southern markets. They stood in rows before the barrels, working in concert, splitting and eviscerating the fish with a rapidity that was perfectly marvellous. Our eyes could scarcely follow the herring as it was caught up from the heap by one woman, who making a cut below the gills, passed it to a second, and she in turn eviscerated it in an instant and handed it to a third who placed it duly between layers of salt in a barrel. It was not pleasant certainly to see so many females, and some were very pretty bright-eyed damsels, up to the elbows in blood and garbage, the refuse of the herring, which was thrown into a heap and rapidly carted away, perfuming the town with no savoury odour as it passed along. Indeed it was almost impossible to stand to leeward of the spot where these operations were being carried on, yet the fair operators seemed healthy and contented, and kept up a ceaseless fire of joke and repartee in their own tongue, for almost all were natives of the Gaelic districts of the West of Scotland.

Shetland 1852

In and around Lerwick

JULY 4th. I calculated that at our ordinary rate of speed, and with a favourable wind, we should be in sight of Sumburgh Head about 5 a.m. At half past five I was upon deck. It was a singularly dull and misty morning, such as might be imagined to be perfectly congenial to the melancholy isles we were approaching. The sea was still rough with the south east breeze that followed the rain of last night, and the sky was obscured by heavy vapours, which hung like a shroud over the leaden coloured waters. The Captain was already on deck, for when do captains ever sleep upon a coasting voyage? And on my enquiring where we were, he pointed to a dark cloud before us somewhat to the left and said that it was Shetland. Fair Isle, which lies midway between Shetland and Orkney, was not yet out of sight, we had passed it some hours before, but it was now partially shrouded in mist, which gave a strange height and aspect to the rocks and the more elevated points of the island. Had the day been clear we should now have distinctly seen both Sumburgh and Fitfield Heads; as it was, the dark cloud before us was the dim outline of Horse Island and of Scatness to the west of the lighthouse, which though 300 feet above the sea was now completely obscured by the fog. Dull as the day was, the atmosphere was warm and wonderfully still, and the Captain predicted fine weather when the sun rose higher above the horizon. I could not withdraw my eyes from the semblance of land – for it was as yet no more – that lay before me, for it was the land I had dreamed of and remembered so warmly, and I watched and peered through the mist for the outline of Fitfield Head, the form of which I had so vividly impressed on my memory, as on a fine summer evening in August 1834 I had looked on it, as I then thought, for the last time and had bid Shetland a long adieu.

By seven o'clock we had entered the famous Roost of Sumburgh, the 'Dynraust' of the old Icelandic historians where about the year 1250 the daughter of Hacon Hakonson, King of Norway, perished with her husband the youthful King of the Western Isles. A terrible sea runs at certain times of the tide through this Roost, as the currents of the Atlantic and German Oceans meet at this point.

When we had passed the entrance of the bay of Sandwick the steamer ran inside of the island of Mousa to land part of the family of Mr Bruce at Sandlodge. They had been our fellow-passengers from Leith, but we had not made acquaintance with them till last evening, when I got into conversation with Mr Bruce's son, a fine spirited youth returning home for the holidays, and full of the sport he anticipated in Shetland. I overheard him describing to his companion, who was evidently a Southron friend, the flights of plovers on the hills, the innumerable snipes in the low lands and the multitude of sea birds on the coast, with all the zest that an English boy would talk of his father's pheasants and hares. The detour of the steamer towards Sandlodge gave us the opportunity of seeing the famous Brough of Mousa, the most perfect remnant now remaining of a mode of fortification peculiar to the north of Scotland and its isles. Mousa has not only an antiquarian but likewise a historic celebrity, for it is more than once alluded to by the Icelandic chroniclers, and stirring events of battle and siege are recorded to have happened around its walls. Standing on a low tongue of land on the isle of Mousa it forms a striking object in the dreary landscape. Its grey and lichen-covered walls are relieved by the brilliant green of the surrounding herbage, while on the low bare island of Mousa there is not a single object to divert the attention from this monument of distant ages; which had seen the first arrival of the Norse Vikings on the Shetland, and still remained nearly perfect four centuries after the Scandinavian rule had ceased in these islands. With our telescopes we could distinguish every stone in its battered walls, as we passed within a musket shot of the shore, and I watched it with the eye of an antiquary till the intervening land shut it off from our sight.

The boat from Sandlodge was waiting for our steamer opposite to the house, which however we could not see till we had rounded the point on our way to Lerwick. Like most of the Shetland lairds' mansions, Sandlodge is of considerable size, and is well protected on the east by the island of Mousa and on the west by the high steep range of hills which runs north and south from Dunrossness. The lower slopes were here clothed with cornfields and grass patches, which seemed to be more carefully tilled and protected than the generality of Shetland enclosures. The absence of hedges, let alone of hedgerow trees, is a great deficit in the Shetland landscape, but in the autumn there is considerable variety in the colours of the cultivated lands, from the intimate admixture of strips of yellow corn with the brilliantly green pasturage. This year the summer was evidently an early one, for not only were the hillsides abundantly clothed with grass, but the corn was well grown and the barley was already in ear on the 4th of July. We were told that few landlords in Shetland have evinced more real solicitude for improving the condition of their tenants than Mr Bruce of Sandlodge, and the fields and enclosures around his mansion bear evidence of the truth of this report. Around the house is a goodly grass garth, the 'graess gaard' of the old Icelanders, but we did not observe much improvement in the houses of the tenants.

By half past nine we were off the south entrance of Bressay Sound. Soon the first houses of Lerwick appeared above the bank, then we recognised Gardie House and the manse of Bressay, and then rounding the South Ness, the steamer dashed at full speed up the well known harbour. All were now on deck admiring the really pretty scene before us. The town of Lerwick lies on a hill sloping rapidly to the water's edge in the form of a crescent, the fort above forms a prominent feature, and at a distance has really an imposing appearance. The harbour itself is one of the finest in the world.[1]

The captain had directed us where to find lodgings, for, as in former days, there is not an inn existing in Lerwick, save one dignified by the name of the Temperance Hotel. When the hurry had somewhat subsided we transferred our luggage into a boat, in company with another tourist whose face was deeply embrowned and blistered by the sun, and pushed off for the shore from which we were only distant about one hundred yards Our fellow passenger proved to be a Mr Yates, a civil engineer from Whitehaven, and an agreeable well informed man. We landed at one of the old worn away stairs, that seemed as if only a few stones had been carelessly piled on the natural surface of the rock, and climbing up some crazy steps, through a narrow alley not four feet wide, we made our way to Mrs Bouwmeester's lodging house, which is one of the best houses in the town. Here, greatly to the astonishment and amusement of my fellow travellers, I was cordially and freely welcomed at the door by a brisk Shetland handmaid, who commenced forthwith a series of questions as to my personal history and the objects I had in view in visiting the distant lands. There was such an air of freedom and of perfectly confident innocence in her questions and deportment, as to contrast strongly with the suspicious looks and short answers of a waiter in a Scottish hotel. Our bulky luggage was soon carried upstairs, while one of us remained below to settle with the boatman. On reaching our bedroom I was greatly amused at finding Caley in the full tide of conversation with the lively handmaid, she pouring forth a volley of questions to which he, seated gravely on a portmanteau in the middle of the room, and perplexed by the volubility of her tongue and the innocent freedom of her manner, made short, but we hope amiable answers. Our bedroom, though almost a garret, was yet extremely comfortable, and so too was the sitting room downstairs, which commanded an excellent view of the harbour.

As we had breakfasted on board and the day was delightfully warm and sunny, I proposed that an excursion should be made to the island of Noss, and to this Mr Yates readily agreed. A boatman was soon found, a ragged poverty-stricken Shetlander, who had been ill for weeks and could hardly crawl on land, but once seated in his boat the poor fellow gained new life and pulled us with great ease across the Sound. The build of the boat, with its high stem and stern, giving it almost a crescentic shape as it sat upon the water, excited the curiosity of my companions. The build of these boats and formerly, if not now, the boats themselves, was imported from Norway, and seems admirably fitted for navigating the narrow voes and islets of these wild coasts. As we rowed across our boatman pointed out a hillock above Gardie House wherein he said a Scottish farmer once preserved ice throughout the whole summer! It was for a bet wi' old Mr Mouat that he did it, said he. Landing at Gardie House we walked past the house and remarked the lilac and other trees rising to the height of the wall but no higher. To my great astonishment when we reached the summit of the first hill we saw before us an excellent road traversing the island in the direction of Noss. I had heard indeed of great improvements having been effected in Shetland in the way of facilities for transit, but I was not prepared for changes so great as we afterwards found to exist in almost all parts of the islands.

The new road through Bressay winds along the hill, and then crosses between two small lakes, stocked with excellent trout, and passes round the southern flank of the eastern hill, which looks upon the island of Noss. Here a man joined us who had evidently been on the look out for steam-boat passengers, many of whom visit the Holm of Noss during the thirty-six hours that they generally spend upon the islands. He offered his services to ferry us over to Noss, which we accepted, and walked on in our company.

The side of Bressay towards the east is steep and rocky, but the grass is peculiarly rich in many parts, though it is difficult for an Englishman to understand how it can bring in to its proprietor, Captain Cameron of Gardie, a rental of not less than five hundred a year. It is evident that the arable and pasture land cannot furnish the half of this sum, but it is in fact derived from the source from whence the Shetland landowners draw their chief riches, from the fisheries in the surrounding ocean.

In the narrow sound over which we were now ferried, the water was beautifully clear, and the bottom was for some distance covered with brilliant white sand, allowing us to discern the smallest object at a considerable depth. Leaping on shore, we walked on through the wide enclosures along a very rough cart road, until we got upon the green pasture, and saw the hill rising up before us, with its outline sharply defined against the blue sky. Our way led us a little to the northwards of the direct line to the Noup or summit, as I wished to bring my companions to a spot whence I knew that the sublime precipices there could be seen in their full majesty. I know few sensations more delightful than that of guiding a friend to view long remembered scenery, which to him is perfectly new and unlooked for. We continued our walk till we reached the eastern side of the island, at the head of a deep but very narrow gio, where the rocks on either side were at least 300 feet in height. Turning towards the south we next crossed a tongue of land, and then sat down within a few inches of the edge of the cliffs, from whence we could enjoy a full view of the magnificent precipices of the Noup. The sun shone here with great power, it was indeed too hot, but to tear ourselves away from the scene before us was impossible.

We now ascended to the highest point of the Noup, climbing with some difficulty up the excessively steep and smooth turf of the northern side of the hill. Near the top a small well of pure cold water was shown to us by a linnet which flew out from beneath the overhanging clump of grass, and here we stopped to eat some oaten cake and smoke our cigars. The green slope of the hill where we stood was covered with an abundance of mushrooms of the finest quality, so that we quickly gathered two handkerchiefs full, but to our surprise, on taking them back to Lerwick, we found that no person there knew how to dress them. They grew in abundance on the fine close turf that forms the southern slope of the Noup, and finer grazing land than this we have rarely seen, and we ceased to wonder that so small an island should in these hyperborean countries bring in to its proprietor the sum of 90 pounds a year.

After descending the southern slope for about 250 feet we found ourselves opposite to the famous Holm of Noss. The Holm is 500 feet in length and 170 in breadth, and few scenes exceed in grandeur this chasm as we viewed it from the point where the well known and oft described cradle is hung. I had frequently visited Noss Island before, but never till this day had found the cradle in its place. A rougher and ruder conveyance across the dark abyss can hardly be imagined. It is a shallow deal box in the form of an inverted table, and strong ropes are passed through holes in the four posts at the corners, and are securely fastened to posts or stakes driven into the ground both on the Holm and on the island. All is solid and well done, there is in reality little danger in the transit, and no accident has ever occurred. As it was Sunday there was little chance of our making the aerial transit, and the cradle was firmly secured by a padlock and chain.

We remained long upon the bank, entranced by the scene and by the genial warmth of the summer's day. At length we turned homewards, and as we were descending to the boat a boy came running to us from the farm house, and requested us, on the part of his mother, to come in and take a drink of milk. We returned, and were most hospitably received in the house where the celebrated Dr Copland was born and where, 18 years before, I had been received by Mr Booth, the father of the present occupier, after a hard and hungry day's shooting on the island of Noss. I mentioned this to our kind hostess, and she appeared to be much gratified that an Englishman should thrice visit the island.

After this we were ferried across the sound, and when we arrived at the grind or gate that separates the common from the enclosed land, we diverged from the former track and diverted our steps towards the manse of the Rev. Mr Hamilton, the Minister of Bressay. Leaving my companions at the pier I walked up to the house and knocking at the door enquired for Mrs Hamilton, whom I had known 20 years ago as Eliza Cameron, and as a fellow passenger on the *Magnus Troil* during our long and dismal quarantine in Bressay Sound. I did not know if I should be recognised by Mrs Hamilton, as she did not know of my intended visit, and might possibly not even remember my name. Mrs Hamilton was at home, said the servant, and I was ushered upstairs to a well furnished drawing room, and after waiting some time, Mr Hamilton's son by a former marriage entered the room and we got into conversation, but it was evident that I was unknown and that my visit was consequently not understood. Mrs Hamiliton was, I was told, not very well, and regretted that she could not see me. I took the hint and after saying a word or two more relating to our former acquaintance in quarantine, I took my leave and in no very amiable humour I walked towards the boat, wondering if I should be received in the same inhospitable manner by all my old friends in Shetland.

I had taken my seat in the boat, and was just beginning to tell of my unsuccessful visit, when young Mr Hamilton rushed in great haste to the pier, and entreated me to return to the manse, as his mother had misunderstood the name I sent in by the servant. The poor fellow seemed so anxious to repair this seeming breach of hospitality that I could not refuse to return, though it was getting late and dinner was waiting for us at Lerwick. I therefore ran back to the house and was most kindly welcomed by Mrs Hamilton, on whom the twenty years that had passed since we last met had left no trace. My visit was a very short one, and promising to call again before we left the country, I returned to my companions in the boat, pulled across the sound, and landed at Lerwick at 4 p.m. in good time for dinner. Several of the younger merchants and employees of Lerwick were, we found, in the habit of dining at the comfortable 'table d'hote' of our lodgings, where the fare was in truth remarkably good. We had soup, fish, roast meat, fowls and rhubarb tart, but neither spirits nor wine were called for, the only drink was weak bottled table beer, a beverage always agreeable but particularly so in the present sultry weather.

After dinner I walked out above the town towards the inlet of Sound, passing Mr Hay's house and some newly built mansions on my right. The whole of the slope of the hill to the south west of Lerwick is covered with villas, with high garden walls to protect the plants and flowers from the cutting blasts of this stormy climate. On the promontory of Sound there are also some neat country houses, whitewashed and roofed with the grey slate of the district. On the other side of the fresh water loch I observed a house actually embowered in trees. The situation is a very sheltered one, and the trees have been planted in a mass and not in belts, so that they have risen even without the aid of high walls to a very respectable height, even to the first floor windows of the mansion they surround. The pastures near Lerwick are fenced in by high and most flimsy stone dykes, enclosing fields where the grass is of a deep olive green colour, for in the low grounds the herbage is rank and slimy, as if the land had been recently recovered from the bed of a small lake.

I remained long on this little islet enjoying the soft beauty of the summer evening and then moved slowly homewards. On the way I was induced to enter a little cabin on the roadside, and it proved to be a good specimen of a Shetland pauper's dwelling. It was so dark that many minutes elapsed before I could discern any objects within through the dense peat smoke that pervaded every part. The only inmate was a poor smoke-dried old woman, seated near miserable peat fire with the never failing accompaniment of a teapot reposing on the hearth. I reached our lodging about half past nine, just as the sun was going down. I entered into conversation with an intelligent young man, a grandson of Mr Thomas Leask of Uyea, my old and worthy friend in former years. We talked of his grandfather and of the many who were now no more, and of the changes that taken place in Shetland properties during the past twenty years. Mr Leask, like his progenitor, was a genuine Shetlander, and had the peculiar pleasing accent of the country in perfection. He told me that he had once been in England, that he had gone as far as Newcastle, and in walking round Eldon Square had seen the name of Dr Charlton on a door, and had recognised it as one of which he had heard often in Shetland. How gladly would he have been welcomed, had he then made himself known to us.

Monday July 5th. Though I was so late in retiring to rest, I rose at an early hour, for my friend Mr Yates wished to make a short boat excursion to the north of the harbour. I was surprised at six a.m. to find so few people in the streets. I soon, however, found that the Shetlanders are not early risers.

Hiring a boat we pushed off to the north end of the harbour against a strong current, to avoid which we kept as close as possible to the western shore. A little beyond Mr Hay's docks we saw some small waders running about amid the seaweed, and landing under cover of a rude breakwater I managed to kill a young Ring Dotterel. Pulling then further to the north we landed upon a small headland exactly opposite to the north entrance to the harbour. I had hoped to have crept up to some gulls and terns that were sitting on the north side of the point, but they were evidently too well accustomed to being pursued by sportsmen, and moved off at my approach. Foiled in our attempt to get some sport here, we pushed across to the north west corner of Bressay Island, and, as we landed there, we were greeted by the shrill cry of the Oyster-Catcher, and saw five of these beautiful birds moving restlessly about on some stones close to the water's edge. In vain, however, did I endeavour to shoot one: they flew backwards and forwards keeping just out of gunshot. We returned over the angle of the island to Hogan, and there regained our boat and rowed back to Lerwick for breakfast.

Our breakfast was as plentiful as our dinner on the preceding day, and after it I spent an hour or two writing letters for the south. I had a long conversation also with two Glasgow merchants who had come to Shetland on a sporting tour. They were hardly, it must be confessed, sportsmen in the true sense of the word, for their whole desire seemed to have been to slaughter hecatombs of inoffensive seafowl, without even the excuse of a predilection for natural history to mitigate their thirst for blood. Having finished my letters I went to call on Mr Charles Duncan, one of the few good fly-fishers in Shetland. To my great regret he was not at home, and I was told that he seldom came into Lerwick before the Monday afternoon. From his house I proceeded to the 'store', for I can give it no other than the American name, of our old and valued friend Mr Hay. I found him at his old post, at the desk where he used to sit in former days, and he received me with the same kind welcome as ever, but how changed was his appearance! In 1832 Mr Hay was the most flourishing, or at least the most enterprising merchant in all Shetland. Fisheries, agriculture and commerce of all kinds were prosecuted by him with an energy that that I have seldom seen equalled, he was as good a specimen as I ever saw of the active-minded Scottish merchant. Since then sorrows and losses had come thickly upon him, his numerous family had died off one by one, his own health had suffered grievously from,

I believe, a stroke of palsy, and his affairs had become so embarrassed that he had been declared a bankrupt. Still under all these afflictions he was now toiling with all the energy and perseverance of a Scotchman to recover his lost ground, and as I was told, with a fair prospect of success. He was now a grey-haired old man, with anxious cares marked deeply on his once handsome countenance, yet there was the same kind voice and the same solicitude to be useful to strangers as I had so fully experienced in former days.

I asked him to procure for us a boat to convey us to Laxavoe on our way to Hillswick, the point we intended if possible to reach this evening. Mr Hay shook his head and said that we could not reach Hillswick that night, but that if we insisted upon it he could find us a boat. This, however, was not, we found, so easy, there was a difficulty at this season of the year in obtaining a crew, and when one was obtained their charges were so exorbitant that my companions were almost in despair. 'A wreck, a boat fare and a drove of whales' are the three Godsends of the Shetlander, and the second of these seemed to be particularly appreciated by the boatmen of Lerwick, who have had their love of gain increased by frequent intercourse with strangers. As soon, however, as they found that one of us was well acquainted with the country, they rapidly lowered their demands, and instead of thirty shillings which they first asked, agreed to take us to Laxavoe for exactly half that sum.

NOTE:
1   Charlton enlarges on its excellence in his journal for July 12, 1832.

Shetland 1852

Making the Most of Hillswick

OUR boat was a small one and pulled only four oars, but proved herself an excellent sailer, and the crew were civil, active and intelligent. At half past twelve we parted from Mr Yates, put our rather bulky luggage on board and, with a fresh south easterly breeze, ran out of the harbour.

The day was remarkably fine, only that a light haze hung over the hills on the mainland. We were soon abreast of the fine point of Rovie Head, where there are the most perfect examples of conglomerate rocks that I ever saw. Beyond this, near to the next point, we observed a green hillock celebrated in the annals of witchcraft as Luggie's Know, or Knoll.[1] Soon after we were nearly abreast of the rock called, I suppose by way of antithesis, the Greenholm, on which with the telescope I saw ten or twelve Eider Ducks and Drakes, sheltering themselves under the lee of the Holm from the rising wind. Beyond Greenholm lies the Soldian rock which in 1832 exhibited a finely perforated arch, but since then it has yielded to the fury of the waves, and not a vestige of the arch remains. The wind had now freshened considerably, and our boat flew over the rising waves, but true to the character she claimed, she shipped not a single sea on our whole passage.

Our crew of four men were, like the rest of their countrymen, very curious about news from the south. One of them however had in his time made a voyage to America, and therefore considered himself well qualified to judge of matters and to lecture his comrades on their ignorance. He told us that a few days before he had witnessed what is surely a rare phenomenon in these latitudes, a waterspout, where the sea was whirled violently round in a small compass, and a portion of the water sucked up into the air to a considerable height. We soon reached the top of the Laxavoe and pushed our boat on shore in a small inlet on its southern banks. As our luggage was being handed out of the boat, the far travelled sailor took possession of my gun and in handing it to me managed to discharge one of the barrels almost in my face. I was somewhat startled, and it might have been a serious accident, but I could not help being amused at the very awkward attempts that were made to impress me that the gun had been fired on purpose lest more damage should ensue[2].

Some women came to us now from the adjoining cottages and offered to carry our luggage over to Voe on the other side of the island. I hesitated and asked if a pony could be procured, for I remembered the heavy portage of our effects in 1834 from Selje to Gruting Voe. I was soon, however, undeceived for I learnt that there was now an excellent road across the island to Olnafirth. About eight women volunteered their services, or rather there were four women, two girls and two smaller children. It was surprising to see what enormous burdens they lifted and carried with ease. Aided by some ropes we had providently brought with us, they soon adjusted the luggage on their shoulders, and all seemed well satisfied with their burdens save one, a poor little girl of about nine years, who seemed brokenhearted at being excluded from our list of porters. We selected for her some trifling parcel, and off she ran in delight to join her companions. Among these was a fair young girl about sixteen years of age with really beautiful features, light hair and bright blue eyes. She had a peculiarly soft Madonna-like expression of countenance, such as I have more than once remarked in Shetland females.

Our porters now set off with the luggage while we determined to skirt the road with our guns, and if possible get some shooting by the way. Caley was a little below me when I heard the well remembered whistle of the Golden Plover and saw a considerable flock of these birds flying across the road and settling a few yards in front of me in my direct path. My old sporting feelings rushed back upon me in full vigour, I crept up to them after the most approved fashion, and succeeded in securing two plump young birds. Had time been allowed we might have killed many more, but we were as yet only half way to Hillswick where we designed to sleep this night.

It was now[3] about 6 p.m., but the sun was still high and bright though there was a certain heaviness in the atmosphere that I could not at the time account for. I was under some anxiety as to whether a boat could be procured here to convey us to Hillswick, for we saw but two anchored in the voe, and one of these was the barge, if I may so term it, of Mr Adie of Voe. To that person's house I accordingly now directed my steps, turning off the main route which ran along the north side of the voe, and descending by a very narrow private road that led towards the mansion. At the head of the inlet was a craggy ravine down which there splashed a rapid stream from the lakes we had passed on our route. On its steep decent were planted no less than three of the picturesque little cornmills which so abound in Shetland, and are indeed so numerous that every little hamlet seems to provide itself with one. Passing some large, well fenced and well cultivated cornfields I proceeded on to Mr Adie's house, while Caley went down with the luggage to the pier. Mr Adie was not at home, but I was kindly received by his wife, who immediately granted me my request for the boat to convey us to Hillswick. Two fine young men offered themselves as our crew, and after a short delay I returned to the pier where the luggage was being placed on the boat.

Caley was seated on the beach surrounded by the whole of our fair portresses from Laxavoe, and engaged in a brisk conversation. We made them quite happy by a present of 2 shillings each, for their heavy portage of four miles. In a few minutes after we were floating on the clear waters of the voe, full of hope that our voyage to Hillswick, a distance of perhaps 18 or 20 miles, would be accomplished before darkness set in. But we had little to fear in this respect, for the utmost darkness at this time of year in ordinary weather is not so obscure as ten o'clock on a June night in the north of England. Breezes light and fitful had now taken the place of the steady south east wind that had been blowing all the morning, and for the first hour we got on well enough. Passing Linga Isle, a desolate brown mass rising from the blue waters, we took to our oars and pulled for the narrow sound that separates Muckle Roe from the Mainland. We could see from here the park walls and enclosures of Busta, the only place in Shetland where trees are said to grow, but the mansion itself was hidden from our view by a projecting tongue of land. Far to the north stretched the inlet of Bustavoe, the scene of the true though tragical story of the vengeance of the Lady of Busta. On its eastern banks we saw many houses of a better class, belonging to smaller proprietors, while the whole of Northmavine, the part we were now about to visit, is the property of Mr Gifford of Busta.

We soon arrived at the narrow channel or Sound of Muckle Roe, a dark, desolate and thinly inhabited island, contrasting strongly with the brilliant green of the hills of Busta. At the entrance to the channel there is a shoal over which even a boat passes with difficulty, so encumbered is it with long filamentous seaweeds, that retard the motion of the boat and cling pertinaciously to the oars. Close to the pointed rock or stack at the entrance to the sound a sloop of Mr Adie's was anchored, having just returned from a successful visit to the cod-fishing banks to the westward of Hillswick. Old recollections here crowded upon me, as I recalled the day in 1834 when, ill of fever and exhausted, I passed Muckle Roe Sound on our way from Papa Stour to Ollaberry. The Sound itself is extremely narrow, in many places it is only a few yards in width, while the banks on either side, though not high, are craggy with intervening glades of very brilliant green pasturage. In the soft calm of this beautiful summer evening we saw numbers of the pretty Black Guillemots seeking their evening meal. I shot also a pretty Kittiwake Gull, which swam wounded to the shore, and in endeavouring to secure the bird we got the boat fast amid the rocks and had some difficulty in extricating it. Our attention had been so engrossed by this chase that we did not notice at first the sudden atmospheric changes that were taking place above us. But when we resumed our oars we heard, far away in the south east, distant and rapidly succeeding peals of thunder, and from the same quarter dark fleecy clouds were hurrying fast over our heads to shut out the sinking sun. There was a singular stillness in the air, even the cries of the seafowl had ceased, as the thunder rolled nearer and nearer.

We were soon out of the Sound and saw before us the broad waters of the Atlantic. Rapidly did the thunderclouds spread over the sky, till the whole was covered save a deep blood-red streak in the west, against which we saw relieved a huge isolated mass, as it were of a gigantic ship in full sail. This I directly recognised as the Drongs, the mighty pinnacles of porphyry that stand out in the sea to the west of Hillswick Ness. Heavy darkness now closed fast upon us, and it became so obscure that we could scarcely see the land, while all around us was still and the sea perfectly calm. The current was against us and it seemed, really, as if we should never get past the mouth of

Gunnester Voe, which we could make out indistinctly by the break in the hills. At length a light breeze sprang up, we hoisted sail, and were soon slipping quietly along under the shadow of the cliffs of Hillswick Ness. As we passed close to the lee of the land, I strained my eyes to recognise the well remembered localities where I had gathered such mineralogical treasures in 1832, but the increasing and extraordinary gloom rendered all objects indistinct. The thunder came nearer and nearer, and at length the storm burst upon us in all its fury. The wind suddenly fell, and a distant pattering sound was heard, a dark irregular line advanced upon us, it was the surface of the hitherto calm sea, splashed up by the enormous raindrops that soon descended on our persons. The darkness now became intense, and was illuminated only by bright flashes of lightning, which revealed for an instant the gaunt forms of the cliffs under which we lay, and were followed directly by peals of the loudest thunder. We could not see ten yards before us, and our boatmen, who were not particularly acquainted with the coast, were almost bewildered by the storm, and appeared uncertain of the course they should pursue. Suddenly we found ourselves close to a projecting low point of peculiar shape, which I instantly recognised as the Taing of Torness, about 300 yards due south of Hillswick House. In a few minutes after, our boat grounded on the beach, the well known beach of porphyry and granite pebbles and boulders, which I had so often traversed on my way to the Ness in 1832. The storm was now at its height, the rain poured in torrents, and though the house was but a few yards distant, we could only discern its outline in the gloom. The lightning and thunder never ceased for a moment, the flashes seemed to play around the mast of our boat, threatening danger directly to ourselves, and indirectly through the gunpowder and loaded firearms that were stowed on board. I jumped on shore, and handing to one of our boatmen a letter for Mr Anderson I covered up the two double barrelled guns with my heavy boatcloak, an old Shetland purchase of mine in 1832, and stood patiently in the tremendous war of the elements until we should be summoned indoors.

It was now about half past midnight, but the household did not seem to have retired to rest. Our boatman soon returned, and along with him came the brother of our future host, and gave us a hearty welcome to Hillswick. No surprise was expressed at our unseasonable intrusion, we might have been expected for weeks, for on entering the house a blazing fire awaited us in the dining room, into which I turned mechanically as to a well remembered room, where I had enjoyed many happy hours.

Could it possibly be twenty years since I had entered that room, and sate at the hospitable table of Thomas Gifford, then the tenant of Hillswick House? Here with an old grey-haired lynx-eyed purser of the Royal Navy I had held hot disputes on religion and politics, for my host was Conservative and anti-Catholic in his opinions, and was not timid in uttering his opinions. And now Thomas Gifford was dead and gone, his amiable wife had died before him, and of his then numerous family, only a single daughter remained, who was an inmate of her uncle's house at Busta.

We were soon furnished with an excellent supper, and enjoyed a long and pleasant conversation with our host's brother. Supper over, I retired to my bedroom, to the room that in old times had been the drawing room, and not a little surprised was I at the elegant modern furniture it contained. An excellent four post mahogany bedstead with all the appropriate furniture of a bedroom, even to scented soap on the washhand stand, made me doubt of my having really reached the extreme point of my hopes and wishes, for it was on Hillswick, its wild and singular coast scenery, its mineral treasures, and wild dark lochs teeming with trout, that my mind had ever been fixed, and now that we were there I could scarcely realise the fact. But the fatigues of this, our first eventful day in Shetland, made me forget the past, and even the thunder without failed to disturb my slumbers.

Tuesday July 6th. Once or twice during the night I was awakened by terrific peals of thunder, which seemed to shake the house to its foundations, but it was only for a moment that my sound sleep was disturbed, and by the morning the storm had passed away. A thick drizzling rain, however, was falling, and the surrounding hills with the Ness itself were obscured by the densest fog. It was ten o'clock before breakfast was ready, but hunger gave a relish to our meal, and we greatly enjoyed the crisp oatcake and the plovers that we had killed yesterday.

About twelve o'clock Mr Gideon Anderson himself appeared and gave us a hearty welcome to Hillswick. He was suffering much from an accident by which his ankle had been injured, and was unable to set his foot to the ground. Having no crutches he had adopted the curious expedient of moving about with his knee upon a chair, and this of course confined his walks to the firm ground upon the beach and the road from the house towards Uriefirth.

I was anxious to procure a pair of 'rivlins' or sandals to wear over my fishing stockings when walking on the moors or wading in the lochs. A shoemaker was soon found and my measure was speedily taken, for he brought out a piece of salted cowhide with the hair on, and placing my foot upon it cut out two square pieces two or three inches longer than my foot and about three times as broad. In ten minutes' time he brought the 'rivlins' in a completed state. The toe end had been sewn up for about two inches, and the same had been done to raise the heel, and a string was then run through the holes made in the sides and the whole was finished. There is some art in tying on the string so that it shall not press upon the foot, but if that is once accomplished there are no chaussures more suitable than these for the mossy hills of the country. As long as the hair, which remains outside, is not worn off, a good footing is always obtained upon the grass.

Thus equipped, and having got ready our fishing rods and guns, we took boat across Hillswick Bay to Hamna Voe. The day was still so heavy and misty that we could not see the Ness of Hillswick, but the rain seemed to be going off. On our way we passed numbers of seabirds. With some difficulty I shot a Razorbill and its young on the smooth waters of Hamna Voe, and I discovered that though I had greatly improved in shooting flying, my skill as a dead shot on the water had greatly declined since my last visit to Shetland. We rowed up nearly to the top of the inlet, and then drawing our boat on shore we crossed a small rivulet and entered one of the cottages to obtain shelter from the rain, which now again came heavily down.

The cottage was of the true Shetland build, and a type of almost all the dwellings throughout that desolate land. It consisted of two rooms, one of which contained a bed and a chair and a most dilapidated table, the other, the kitchen, seemed to be the general dwelling place of the family. The floors of both these rooms were merely of hardened earth, and in the centre of the kitchen was a small fire of peats, the smoke from which escaped through an opening in the roof. The furniture consisted of sea chests ranged round the room and one rickety cupboard, and above these were piled fishing lines, articles of clothing and old 'cassies' (straw baskets) with articles of clothing; all in admirable confusion and thoroughly begrimed with peat smoke. The poor widow who occupied the cottage was in great distress, as she had just received the news of the death of her son at the Davis Straits fishery. She told us that a year or two before she had lost two fine boys at the very loch to which we were bound that day. They had been attempting to reach an islet or holm in the loch by wading, and probably by holding on each other's hands one had slipped into deep water and had dragged his brother in after him. Some neighbours came in while we were there to comfort the poor widow, and they kept up a melancholy conversation in a singularly plaintive tone of voice. An old man of 86, the father-in-law of the widow, came down from the cottages above through the pouring rain, and greatly interested us by his intelligent conversation, while our fishing tackle and rods much attracted his attention. The old Shetlander, like most of his countrymen, was anxious to hear all the news from the south, and made many enquiries about the railroads and the wonders of the electric telegraph. The poor widow brought us a bowl of bland, which I persuaded Caley to taste, but he would not drink and vowed that it was the most detestable liquor in the world. I had certainly tasted better bland in former years, or else my palate had grown more delicate.

The rain still continued, but at about 3 p.m. I declared that I would wait no longer, and taking our rods we walked up the burn towards the lake which was distant about a mile from the house. The ascent was steep and rugged, but I found that my 'rivlins' answered their purpose well, and further experience made me walk quite easily in them. We soon neared the banks of the loch, and saw before us, embosomed in dark heathery hills a fine piece of water about a mile in length by half a mile broad. There was a holm of considerable size near its centre, and on it was established the usual colony of Black-backed Gulls. I was myself quite a novice in loch fishing, for twenty years I had never tried anything but the streams of Northumberland. It was therefore with a palpitating heart, and with all the eagerness of a young sportsman on the 12th of August, that I proceeded to tie on two of James Wilson's[1] largest and most attractive loch-flies, The Greenmantle and the Grizzly-king, and marching into the loch to the edge of the deep water I commenced my labours. My first half dozen throws were unsuccessful, but at the next I felt a dead heavy pull which showed I had hooked a weighty fish. He resisted my efforts for some time to bring him to shore, but at length I got him within reach of the landing net and laid him on the grass to contemplate at leisure his beautiful proportions. He was a full short powerfully built fish of something more than a pound in weight, and exquisitely bright in colour. A few minutes after I hooked another, but in a critical plunge I injudiciously slackened the line and he escaped. Caley was not inclined to fish, but wandered off with his gun towards the south bay of the loch, where two of the Red-throated Divers were reposing upon the water. I now crossed the shallow stream that ran from the loch and continued along the banks. Almost immediately a fine fish rose and after five minutes' play was landed. He was bulkier than the other and much more powerful in his struggles, his weight would be under a pound and a half. Both these fish took the Greenmantle fly. The rain now interfered to spoil my sport, it came down in torrents and the fish gave over feeding.

About 7 p.m. the rain cleared off, but the wind also went down and the surface of the loch became bright and smooth as a mirror. As we came down to the boat a Grey Crow rose from it and was ineffectually fired at by Caley. We found that the rapacious thief had been feasting on the birds we had left in the boat, and had almost torn them to pieces. The night was damp and misty but our crew predicted fair weather for the morrow. We arrived at Hillswick about 9 p.m., and our trout when cooked for supper proved to be most delicious. They were deep coloured as salmon, and fully equal to that fish in flavour. Mrs Anderson joined us at tea. She remembered my former visit, and spoke much of her father and of her good old uncle Arthur Cheyne of Ollaberry.

Wednesday July 7th. The exercise of yesterday had been so trivial that it only served to prepare us for more active work today. At 6 a.m. I was ready to go out onto the Ness of Hillswick. Twenty years before I had issued from the same gates upon the same expedition, and well do I remember the fearful day of wind and rain that I devoted to exploring the geology of the Ness. Today I bore on my shoulders the identical geological bag, and carried in my hands the same geological hammer that I had then used, and both felt to me like old acquaintances who had returned after long years of separation.

I had a pretty accurate idea of the configuration of the promontory, though I had seen but little of it in the rain and fog of 1832. On my left was the low promontory of Torness Taing, it was as green and fresh as if buildings had once stood upon it, but no traces of ruins remain. On this point is a beautiful vein of claystone porphyry, on which a polished specimen now lies before me. Beyond the Ness of Thor is a small gio into which trickles a tiny stream from a miniature lake above. Beyond this the horneblende slate rock is thrown into the wildest confusion by the irruption of veins of porphyry. From hence I pursued my course towards the south end of the Ness. I knew that the Queen Gio, where the garnets were so plentiful, lay on the east side of the Ness, but the mist and rain of 1832 had prevented me from noting the exact locality. Ascending a considerable rise I came again on a deep still gio where the water was sleeping calm and bright in the sun that was now beginning to disperse the heavy mist. Here the rocks had changed their character and exhibited on the southern side a lighter colour and a totally different fracture on their sea face. On the north side of this gio was a fine vein of brick red porphyry which contrasted strongly with the greyish white hue of the rocks through which it had burst. Climbing the next height I saw before me a cliff glittering brightly in the sunshine, and immediately I recognised it as the garnet-bearing mica slate.

Every portion of the rock was studded thickly with garnets, from the smaller ones of the size of peas to the fine well crystallised dodecahedrons so large as filberts. The matrix was a white pearly mica slate, which shivered pretty easily in one direction and left the garnets standing out on the surface in high relief. There had been other visitors to the garnet cliffs since I had been there in 1832, for I found some pretty fresh specimens lying about, but they were not cleanly dressed off, and were evidently the work of a young hand. I remained nearly two hours on this sunny spot, gazing into the clear water beneath, and calling up memories of old times and scenes connected with Hillswick. For years I had dreamed of returning to this very spot; in 1834 I had reached as far as Ollaberry only four miles distant, and was then overtaken by sickness and had to retrace my steps. Since then I had looked on all chance of revisiting Hillswick as visionary, and now, thank God, I was once more in my favourite haunts, and felt all that vigour of health and fresh hearty enthusiasm which spurred me to exertion twenty years before.

It was now near nine o'clock, and with my geological bag filled with choice specimens, and my pockets too laden to the utmost, I returned leisurely over the short yielding turf of the Ness to Hillswick. I knew there was no call for speed, breakfast would not be ready till ten o'clock, for they are very late in Shetland. It is true that they are very tardy in going to bed, at Hillswick the whole population was on foot till midnight, and it was sometimes an hour past that time before the buith or store was closed. The extreme beauty and calm of the summer nights, the habit of remaining out at piltock fishing till 10 or 11 p.m., all tend to induce late hours in these northern latitudes. He that would go to bed and rise again with the sun would have short night's rest in the Shetland summer. It might be expected that these habits would be reversed in winter, but such is not the case. In December the daylight is gone even in clear weather by 4 p.m., and then the Shetlanders, like their Norwegian forefathers, congregate around the peat fires of their cottages, and by the light of a rude oil lamp pursue their indoor occupations and tell long stories of perilous adventures by sea and land.

The day was now remarkably fine, and Mr Anderson had ordered a boat to be in readiness at Sandwick, on the west side of the Ness, to convey us to Stenness. Taking our guns and some light provision we walked across the low neck of land that connects the Ness of Hillswick with Northmavine. It is only two or three hundred yards across, and then we came to a high beach of sand on which our boat was resting. It was a small craft and somewhat old, nor did the crew consist of young men, but they were the most daring boatmen we ever saw, even in Northmavine which supplies the best and most enterprising crews for the Shetland fishery.

We pulled out of the sandy bay and rowed quietly along the western side of the Ness towards some high stacks or rocky pinnacles which when seen from the land are exceedingly pictureque. Of these the huge mass of the Drongs ('Drengerne,' 'the Giants') is by far the most remarkable. Their perpendicular sides have never been scaled by man. Seen from Hillswick Ness, the Drongs present their broadsides to the shore, and appear as outworks thrown up to arrest the ravages of the ocean. From their northern or southern extremities they present the most fantastic forms, of pillars, pinnacles and buttresses, all in rich colours of deep red, green and white. The day was so calm that we were enabled to row close in to these huge rocks, and could even have landed on their shelving base.

Leaving the Drongs we hoisted sail and steered due west with a light breeze. Some heavy mist still lay on the water, and it was long before we could make out the island of Doreholm, towards which we were now directing our course. Doreholm lies about a mile from the shore and nearly opposite to the house of Tangwick. Rounding the northern side of the island we came in sight of the magnificent archway in the cliff which has probably given the island its peculiar name. A rocky promontory is here cut through by the waves into an archway of the height of 80 to 90 feet, and wide enough at the base to allow a good sized boat to pass. There was rather a heavy ground swell rolling in from the Atlantic today, and the waves beat so heavily on the cliffs that I did not care to venture very near them, though our daring crew was quite ready to make the attempt. Leaving Doreholm we directed our course towards Stenness, the most westerly point of the peninsula of Northmavine.

It was now about 2 p.m. and the mist began to clear way, as we entered the narrow channel between the Holm of Stenness and the island of that name. Suddenly a boat dashed out of the mist, filled with the well remembered forms of the fishermen. There was the red nightcap of the father of the family and the gaily coloured woollen caps of the young men; but I looked in vain for the old skin coat, without which few men went to sea in 1832. There was not one now to be seen, the mackintosh coat and oiled canvas jacket had effectually replaced this old relic of Scandinavia, and the Shetland skin dress must now be sought for further north, in the isles of Faroe or among the Loffodens. Perhaps a few still linger in North Yell, but I could not find a single one at Stenness. Boat after boat now followed, and it was evident that the fishermen were going out to the far Haaf or most distant fishing ground, at least thirty miles from the land. One boat, the first we met, passed very near us, and I strained my eyes to catch a well remembered face, that of Lawrence Robertson, my old companion at Hillswick. Strange to say he was really, as I afterwards found, in this very boat, but 20 years, which had worked little change in me, had altered Laurie Robertson to a red-faced grizzle-bearded old man.

We now turned our boat into the strait between Stenness Island and the mainland, and landed upon the former to pursue the Oyster-Catchers and Terns. We shot one or two of the loudly piping Oyster-Catchers as they skimmed over our heads, and where they fell hundreds of terns congregated in the air and almost deafened us with their cries. The cattle were larger and better fed here than in any other part of the islands, and the rich food had made them bold and dangerous. One of them, separating from the rest, approached me with evidently hostile intention, so that I thought it prudent to entrench myself on the top of a huge boulder of rock, where there was hardly room to stand. The animal seemed surprised at my sudden elevation, and remained pawing the ground at about ten yards' distance. While in this position an Oyster-Catcher flew over my head, and offered such a tempting shot that I fired when the bird was directly above me. The recoil of the gun threw me off my balance, and it was with the utmost difficulty that I escaped a severe fall. The report of my gun, however, totally discomfited my enemy, and when I recovered my balance I saw him careering wildly across the island towards the rest of the herd. With many birds of various species in our boat we now pulled across the bay to the fishing hamlet of Stenness.

On the stony beach was a long array of boats, interspersed with square piles of fish in various stages of curing, while huge wooden troughs for salting, sea boots, waterproof jackets and fishing gear were lying around. The beach at Stenness was exactly that which is best adapted for the process of fish curing, the large round stones of which it was composed admitting of a free current of air beneath the piles of fish, while the wet was carried speedily away in the interstices of the stones. In the centre of the beach rose the two storied 'bude' or buith, the store house for the fishermen, and the temporary abode of the factor. On either side of this house were ranged irregular rows and clusters of huts, curious turf-covered cabins, with walls constructed of uncemented stones, and roofs of turf; the dwellings of the fishermen during their sojourn at the station in the fishing season. We entered one or two of these cabins and in one of them found some men who had just returned from the deep sea fishing. There was a turf fire in the centre of the low hut, the smoke from which escaped by a hole in the roof, and the atmosphere was close and stifling. For all this, these men are in general healthy, and I believe they are more temperate than formerly, consuming more of coffee and of tea than of whisky.

We left the boat here and set off on foot to walk over the 'Villians of Ure' to the 'Grind of the Navir'. We soon arrived at the enclosure of the Cross Kirk, once so famous for the pilgrims that resorted to it in Catholic times. The churchyard, which is still used as a burial place, is surrounded by a good substantial wall, but of the famous kirk itself scarcely a vestige remains. Sir Henry Dryden, who visited the Cross Kirk about a month after we were there, informs me that he could make nothing of the outlines of the church, and that he does not think that it stood in the burying ground but at a little distance to the east where there are the remains of some strong and thick walls. We must not forget, however, that in all probability the Cross Kirk was utterly destroyed by the zealot Mr Hercules Sinclair, sometime, as old Brand tells us, minister in Northmavine:

> He, in his zeal against superstition, rased Cross Kirk in this parish because the people superstitiously frequented it. And, when demolished, behind the place where the altar stood, and also beneath the pulpit, were found several pieces of silver of various shapes, brought thither as offerings by afflicted people, some being in the form of a head, others of an arm, others of a foot, accordingly as the offerers were distressed in these parts of the body. (*Description of Zetland*, 1701, p.95.)

I suspect the ruins outside the kirkyard were possibly those of the presbytery.

The mist now began to clear fast away, and we found ourselves on the eastern slope of a green hill, looking down on a large, placid lake. From the loch we followed the course of a little streamlet that seemed to run towards the rising green bank on the west. It was sufficiently strong to turn the wheels of three picturesque little Shetland mills that were situated on its course. Just below the last mill the stream disappeared, and as we approached the spot we saw, opening before us in the greensward, a hideous chasm with the still waters of the ocean at the bottom. There were two of these perforations, each about 100 feet in depth, the first, or that nearest to the sea, with perfectly perpendicular sides, the second, which is 250 feet from the sea, is shelving at its eastern extremity, where the stream enters from the lake, so that a good climber might possibly make his way down to the bottom. It was most curious to look through the archways of this tremendous rift, and to see the tiny blue waves agitated by the sea without breaking on the shingle below. This we could do by creeping close to the edge of the cliff over which the stream from the loch descended in a tiny waterfall, and then we looked under the first archway till the gloomy cavern seemed to close down over the water.

Leaving this spot we proceeded straight to the cliffs to search for the Barn of Scradda, a cavern in the face of the cliff which in wartime often afforded a shelter for the hunted fishermen from the pursuit of the press-gangs. I had visited this cave in 1832,[5] but could not remember its exact position. Laurie Robertson, who then guided me, knew the place well, and feelingly described to me the sufferings of the poor men, as they huddled together in the cave during the long winter's nights, not daring to light a fire for fear of their retreat being discovered. Our man today hardly knew the spot, but we walked up to a sheepfold on the brink of the cliff which he remembered was in its immediate vicinity. Our conductor then led us to the point of a steep bare rock amid a wilderness of gios and dark frowning precipices Pointing to a ledge about 30 feet below, he said it was directly in front of the cavern, and taking off his shoes, he made his way down with some difficulty. Caley followed him down the steep and slippery rock, but as I had seen the cave before and knew that it presented no peculiar features, I did not choose to risk my neck by a second descent. On his return Caley showed himself a good cragsman by scaling the rock with great alacrity, and I thought he looked well pleased when he had reached the summit.

Our way now led us northwards. We soon came abreast of the Maiden Skerry, an isolated rock with such absolutely perpendicular sides that it has never yet been scaled. North of the Maiden Skerry we observed two seals, the first we had seen on this visit. Crossing another portion of greensward we came to the Grind of the Navir. The mist had now quite cleared away except far off out to sea where it hung over the island of Foula, and adhered so closely to the high precipices there that, though but a cloud, it formed a correct outline of that singular isle. We enjoyed the warm afternoon's sunshine after the mist and the bright gleams that glittered on the smooth ocean, gilding the wild rocks of Ossa Skerry, and tinting the green swelling hills towards Hamna Voe and the bright red granite precipices at the back of Roeness Hill. It was now about 5 p.m., and we returned to Stenness, where we were regaled with tea and cold tusk fish in the house of the factor. We then re-entered our boat and with a soft west wind glided smoothly along the coast towards Hillswick.

It was 8 p.m. when we arrived at Hillswick, but the bright light of these northern latitudes showed us that we had several hours still of day. We therefore determined to go to the head of the Uriefirth Voe to a loch where we were told there were a considerable number of trout. A sharp walk along the new road from Hillswick to Lerwick brought us to the wished for spot. The surface of the small lake was calm and smooth as a polished mirror, and not a fish stirred. A poor ragged lad whom I had seen at Hillswick in the morning now came timidly up to me, and advised me to go further along the banks to a point where the water was deeper. About nine o'clock the trout began to rise freely, particularly around a heap of stones in the loch, said to be the remains of a brough. I did not get any large trout, but many of fair size, though they were much inferior both in beauty of shape and in flavour to the Pundswater trout. It was half past ten before we left the loch, and there seemed to be even then no diminution of the daylight, though the sun had then set.

Thursday July 8th. At a very early hour in the morning a boy brought me a letter by express from Busta, which had arrived there by the post late in the preceding night. I felt greatly puzzled at first, I had thought myself in Shetland perfectly clear of all express messages, but on opening the letter I found it was from Mr Charles Duncan of Lerwick, the most enthusiastic and the most successful fly-fisher in all Shetland. In his note he gave me all the information he could relative to the Northmavine lochs, but he had not fished much in that part of the country.

At 7 a.m. I was told that Lawrence Robertson, my old guide at Hillswick, had come over from Stenness to see me. Poor Laurie was indeed delighted to see me, but I should hardly have recognised, in the grey-headed red faced old man, the stout young fellow who accompanied me in 1832. I fear that Laurie is not quite so temperate a man as he should be, but he had the same open countenance and pleasant mild way of talking as before. I was not able to spend a day again upon the Ness, as we were going to Helgawater to fish, but I commissioned Laurie to go to the well known localities and to procure some additional specimens.

About 11 a.m., for it was impossible to get away sooner, we set off round the head of St Magnus Bay, and followed the road past the loch at Uriefirth where we had fished the night before. Our guide was the intelligent lad who had joined us the evening before at Uriefirth loch; he was miserably clad, even for a Shetlander, and besides suffering from scrofula he had yesterday cut his foot severely by treading on an adze. We now saw before us the whole expanse of Helgawater, it is a larger loch than Pundswater, but the surrounding hills are much less picturesque in their outline. After preparing our tackle we separated, and Caley took the west side of the loch, while I went along its southern banks. I soon raised and hooked three or four goodly fish and with the assistance of the boy landed them in safety.

On examining our provender we found we were most scantily provided with food, and I bethought myself of dispatching our attendant to Ollaberry to procure some bread and cheese at the buith there. It seemed most strange to me to send a messenger to Ollaberry, a place which was so strongly impressed upon my memory by the events that occurred there in former years. Arthur Cheyne was now no more, his estate was a wreck, and was advertised for sale. During the famine years of 1847-1848 Mr Cheyne expended large sums in purchasing potatoes and meal for his starving tenantry, while he demanded no rent from them, and the poor people feared that they had become helplessly involved. At their good landlord's death in 1850 it was found that all outstanding arrears of rent had been cancelled in his books, he had not thought of his own interests, and the sale of his estate barely paid his debts. Our little messenger expressed his doubts of finding any provision at Ollaberry, but he cheerfully undertook the journey and we saw him climb the hill to the eastward, beyond which lay the enclosed ground of Ollaberry. It was an hour or two before he returned, and he came back empty handed, there were no provisions at the store, nothing, indeed, but a small quantity of whisky. We did not much care, we had some oatcake in our pockets, and we had the more time to devote to fishing.

About nine o'clock hunger conquered our love of sport, and we turned homewards carrying our guns and heavy baskets of fish. When we reached Hillswick we found Laurie Robertson who had returned from Hillswick Ness with a cassie full of indifferent specimens; he had not succeeded in procuring a single piece of actinolite or rhaetizite, minerals that used to be plentiful there. We found the Helgawater trout delicious, but not so red in flesh as those we had taken in Pundwater two days before.

NOTES:

1   Luggie was a wizard whose miraculous skill at fishing caused him to be burnt for witchraft near Scalloway, according to a passage in Brand quoted by E.C.

2   The boatman may have had a case. Presumably Charlton had loaded his gun in the hope of shooting birds on the way, but he should have unloaded it before landing.

3   When they reached Olnafirth, several miles and golden plovers further.

4   James Wilson was an Edinburgh fishing friend.

5   Journal for September 11th.

Shetland 1852

Last Days in Shetland

SATURDAY July 10th[1]. We were employed during the early part of this morning in packing up our rather weighty baggage, preparatory to our departure for Lerwick. The poor lad Andrew, who had been our companion and guide during the last three days, wore today an air of settled grief upon his countenance; he asked me in a low enquiring tone to come back next year, and he would show me some beautiful rocks upon Roeness Hill. He had got another thunderbolt[2] for me today, and promised to find many more if I would only come next year. Our heavy portmanteaux had been sent off two days before by the trading sloop, but this mode of conveyance is not a rapid one, for we reached Lerwick before the sloop came in.

At eleven o'clock we took leave of Mr Anderson and his wife, by whom we had been most hospitably entertained, and walked across the isthmus to Sandwick Bay, where our boat was lying. The wind blew stiffly from the south west, the sky in that quarter was dark and lowering, and our boatmen foretold a gale. They felt no apprehension, however, at the prospect; we should reach smooth water, they said, before the gale could rise. Our boat was small and old, I should have preferred certainly a six-oared deep-sea fishing boat and a younger crew, but we found that though three of our men were advanced in years, they had lost none of that daring spirit for which the Northmavine men are so famous. Having placed our luggage, including two cassies full of minerals, beneath the thwarts of the boat, we embarqued, and along with us Mr Hendrie, an active Queen's Messenger of Lerwick.

As we left the bay and pulled out for the Drongs we saw several seals sporting on the troubled waters, but the unsteady motion of the boat prevented us from getting a shot. As we neared the Drongs it was evident that the wind and sea were rising fast, and the heavy waves of the Atlantic dashed with a thundering sound against these porphyry barriers. I was at first at a loss to understand why our boatmen should seek so large an offing, but they knew the currents and the set of the tide better than we did, and the boat was not well fitted to encounter the heavy seas close in shore. At length when we had got through the seething green water directly south of the Drongs, we laid in the oars, hoisted our sail, and steered for the opening of Muckle Roe Sound. Old Andrew took the helm, and Magnus, the youngest of the crew, stood by the sail, holding the halyards, while the sheet was in the hands of the helmsman. The wonderful powers of sailing exhibited by the Shetland build of boats is well known. When steering the helmsman sits so low, upon a small semicircular piece of wood inserted in the sharp stern of the boat, that he steers with the tiller over his shoulder, and in rapidly shifting the tiller to meet an advancing wave, he merely lowers his head and shifts the tiller over to the other side without moving from his seat. The advantages of this position are obvious, there is little or no danger of the helmsman being struck from his seat by the heaviest wave, and with the sheet in his left hand he commands the sail in any sudden squall.

And now the waves rose fast and furious, though the wind never fortunately increased to a gale, but we were no doubt on the edge of a storm the full force of which never reached us. Still there was a heavy sea, such a sea as I had not encountered since my last expedition to this country, but the old crazy boat behaved admirably, and the crew did their work to perfection. As we neared the Longhead we saw the waves breaking furiously upon its tremendous precipices, and it was obvious too that on our present tack we could not weather the Head. On, however, we went, and every minute the sea became rougher, till even the crew looked anxious, for our old boat strained and creaked in every plank, as though she would part asunder. Many a heavy wave now dashed its crest into the boat, drenching us all, but particularly Caley who sat on the weather side, and requiring active exertion in bailing out the boat. Nearer and nearer we approached the cliffs, and so high were the huge waves setting in from the open Atlantic, that at times when the boat was in the trough of the sea the land was entirely hidden from our sight. Still our resolute boatmen held on their course, till we were almost in the broken water at the foot of the precipices. Just then a heavier sea than ordinary broke immediately to seaward of the boat, and drenched us all most impartially with its spray, but elicited no further remark from the crew that the simple exclamation to the steersman 'Andro! You're weeting de gentlemen!' Magnus meanwhile kept a sharp look-out ahead and suddenly exclaimed 'Luik out! Andro, luik out! There's a hantle o juimp ahead!' Andrew braced himself for the trial, and ducked his head with extraordinary agility beneath the tiller as he guided the boat through the raging seas, and then cried to Magnus to 'Doun da seil wi' grit care.' Down went the sail and the boat's head flew up to the wind, while the men leaped to the oars, and in a minute we were pulling out to sea, tilting lightly over the waves and hardly shipping a drop of water. For about half an hour we continued to make an offing, and then we hoisted sail and ran under the lee of Muckle Roe into smooth water. We were just in time, had we been an hour later in starting we could not have crossed Hillswick Bay in a six oared boat.

Though on entering Muckle Roe Sound we got into perfectly smooth water, yet in this narrow passage we were not entirely free from perils, for the dangerous 'flanns' or blasts of wind swept down with resistless force through every gully. Magnus therefore kept his place beside the mast holding the halyards ready to lower sail on the instant that a squall approached. Onwards we now sped quickly, dividing the dark still waters of the Sound, the wind aloft impelled our sails, but in the boat we felt it not, as the high cliffs on either side effectually screened us. We now approached the eastern entrance of the Sound, and held a council among ourselves as to whether we should run on as originally planned up to the head of Aithsvoe, and cross from thence to Bigsetter Voe, taking boat from thence to Scalloway, or continue on to Olnafirth, and find our way from thence direct to Lerwick. Mr Hendrie, who was well acquainted with the country, strongly advised us to adopt the latter course, as it was more than doubtful whether we should find a boat at Bigsetter Voe, or at least a crew to man it, as all the men were absent at the deep sea fishing. He said too that the sea, from the direction of the wind, would be extremely heavy in crossing the mouths of Weesdale and Whiteness Voes. We therefore decided to run to Mr Adie's house at Olnafirth, and there to procure a cart or ponies to convey our luggage to Lerwick.

Pursuant to this resolution we again hoisted sail and steered for Olnafirth, but we found our progress wonderfully retarded by some unseen obstacle. The breeze filled our sails and ruffled the surface of the water, but the boat hardly moved at all. We thought of the mermaids and the Kraken, of the trows that Brand speaks of, 'great rolling creatures that doe disturb the boats,' and of the other spirits that live beneath the great waters. It was none of these, for on looking over the stern we saw that we dragged behind us a long train of beautiful seaweed, over a bed of which we had passed when crossing the shallows at the east end of Muckle Roe Sound.

Once freed from the mass of weeds, the boat sprung over the smooth water with extreme rapidity, though it was necessary still to keep a man at the halyards as the squalls increased in violence as we approached the head of Olnafirth Voe. About 2 p.m. we landed at Mr Adie's quay, and after depositing our luggage on the beach, we walked up to the house to engage a conveyance for our things to Lerwick. We found Mr Adie busily engaged in his store, but he assured us that he would get our luggage forward to Lerwick by some means or other that night, though both carts and men were difficult to be obtained at this season. We therefore determined to push on at once on foot the whole distance of nineteen miles, leaving our luggage to be forwarded as Mr Adie should arrange.

Taking leave of our Hillswick crew, we breasted the hill near the waterfalls, and soon joined the main road from Hillswick to Lerwick. Mr Hendrie, though somewhat advanced in years, was an excellent pedestrian, and after we had passed the road that comes in from Laxavoe, we set our faces fairly towards the south, and at a rattling pace proceeded along the excellent road.

I was glad of the opportunity of seeing more of the inland communications that have recently been opened out in Shetland. The road, though narrow, was excellently engineered,[3] but I remarked that the embankments were often merely raised of turf, a material that will only last a few years. Still there is abundance of good material close at hand, and they can be repaired and kept up at a very small expense. Some of the bridges over the gullies were narrow and very slightly built, but in general the line must have been very easy of construction. The afternoon gradually improved, we had only a few showers, and the wind abated by about 7 p.m.

We had made good way for the first three hours, never relaxing our pace, and by that time we had advanced twelve miles on our journey.

Passing the loch of Girlsta we halted for a short time at the house of the schoolmaster at Wadbuster, where we were treated with whisky and milk in true hospitable fashion. On leaving this place I stopped at a loch at the head of Wadbuster Voe and tried a few throws for trout as the evening was very fine, but could only get a few rises, and the fish seemed small and scarce. Over a gentle rise the road now led us into the fine and well cultivated valley of Laxfirth, where agriculture seems to have made more progress than in any other part of Shetland. Here were large well laid out fields, surrounded by well built dykes, and the Scotch system of husbandry seemed to be diligently followed. It was now late, about 9 p.m., for we had lingered much on this latter part of our journey, when I bethought me of calling on Mr Charles Duncan, the brother angler who had so kindly written to me when at Hillswick, and who resided in this fine valley at his country house of Gott (Gode). We soon made out his abode, and though it was now nine in the evening, we did not hesitate about calling on him, as we were certain, in this hospitable country, of meeting with a kind reception. In a few minutes we were seated by a comfortable fire, discussing the merits of various flies and of many and various lochs, in a strain of enthusiasm and earnestness unknown to all but anglers. True to his tastes he had located himself in this comfortable little mansion, situated between the loch of Tingwall and the Strandloch, both of which are famous for trout and both within an easy walk.

For supper we had this evening some of the delicious Tingwall trout, which Mr D. had captured an hour or two before in the loch. They were short plump fish about half a pound in weight, and exquisitely flavoured. Over an ample supply of cigars and toddy we prolonged our sitting far into the night, indeed I fear we encroached so much upon the Scottish Sabbath, that had it been known, our friend might have been brought up before the Kirk Sessions for keeping of unlawful hours on the Sabbath morning. Late hours and whisky toddy are, however, common enough on Sabbath afternoons in Scotland.

Mr Duncan when we parted 'a wee short hour ayont the twal', insisted that one of us should ride his pony into Lerwick. Caley was somewhat fatigued with the long walk from Olnafirth, and he accordingly accepted the kind offer, while I walked beside him for the remaining five miles of the journey. When we reached Lerwick the people were still in the streets, though it was now 3 a.m., and we found that our luggage had already arrived, having been carried by two men and three women all the way from Olnafirth.

Sunday July 11th. During the morning we walked out to the west of the town, and about one o'clock we rowed across Bressay Sound to Gardie, to call upon the Rev. Mr Hamilton. He was delighted to see us, and we found him the same intelligent and amiable man as he is represented by Ployen in his admirable book on Shetland. One of my great objects was to see a stone which I had been informed was in Mr Hamilton's possession, and which according to the account I had received from Mr W.H. Fotheringham of Kirkwall, had a runic inscription engraved upon it. Mr Fotheringham had never seen the stone in question, he had only heard of its existence. On asking Mr Hamilton about it, he said there was certainly a carved stone in the croft behind the manse, but he was not aware that it bore any inscription, except some rude lines upon the edge, which might possibly be an inscription. He accordingly conducted us to the Garth, and there reared against the wall was a slab of chlorite slate covered with most curious carvings, but without any trace of runic inscription. On the edges, however, I saw lines deeply cut across, and in an instant the truth flashed upon me, that it was an Ogham inscription on a headstone of the true Irish or Scots-Irish character. Of its Christian origin there could be no doubt, the crosses and figures upon it plainly showed this to be the case. Perhaps, and indeed in all probability, the remarkable stone had been erected when the Papae, or Western Christians, ruled in Shetland before the advent of the Norsemen, and consequently it would not be less than 1000 years old. That it had been a headstone there was not doubt, and in all probability it had stood at the head of another stone placed in a horizontal position, as the carving on the one side descends much lower than on the other. This discovery alone would have been worth the long journey to Shetland. This stone had been found some years ago at the ruined church of Cullensbro' in Bressay, and was from thence transferred to Gardie House in the time of the late Mr Mouat of Garth. At parting we promised to return the next day to dinner, an engagement which, however, we were unable to fulfil.

On our return to Lerwick we joined a pleasant party at dinner at Mrs Bouwmeester's boarding house. One of the gentlemen present proved to be the factor of Dr Scott of Vailey, the successor of the venerable Mr Scott of Vailey who had died a year or two ago at the patriarchal age of ninety two. The factor had been in Foula only a week before, and I was glad to hear of my old friends on that wild island, of Mr Petersen and of Lawrence Ratter the intelligent islander who accompanied us to Papa Stour.

After an excellent dinner we walked out along the road to Sound in a lovely evening, soft and mild as in Italy in April[1], and with the additional advantage of an indefinitely prolonged twilight. Two of our party had that morning walked as far as the Brough of Brinnastir about six miles to the south of Lerwick, and from their description of this stronghold it would seem that some of the lower apartments in the concentric walls are still in a very good state of preservation. About half past nine we assembled at tea, and the conversation took a singular turn, viz on the Achilli trial, which seemed to have excited great interest among the Scotch. I was gratified to find that, with the exception of one sour-looking Presbyterian, all the rest of the company was convinced of the apostate Italian's guilt, and regarded the behaviour of Lord Campbell and the verdict given as a deep stain on the administration of justice in England.

Monday July 12th. We were in some doubt this morning as to whether we should remain another week in Shetland or should return to Scotland by the steamboat that sailed this afternoon at six o'clock, and after due consideration we decided to adopt the latter plan, as no letters had come by this week's boat, and we hoped to find some in Orkney. Having packed up the greater part of our luggage we set off at 8 a.m. to walk to Tingwall and to enjoy a few hours' angling there before we finally left Shetland.

The day was so close that at first we both felt inclined to lie at full length on the soft turf rather than try our fortune on the glassy surface of the loch. However at length I got Caley to go up to the manse to obtain permission from the minister to use one of his boats, while I busied myself in preparing the fishing tackle. I tried a few casts from the bank but could raise no fish, and I did not like to wade, having left my fishing boots in Lerwick. The shore shelved too gradually at this point for me to reach the deep water where the fish are generally to be found, but I now saw Caley pulling the boat along the loch, and we were soon floating on its waters. The surface was perfectly smooth, as there was not the slightest breeze, and we tried all manner of tempting flies without the least success. Caley then suggested we should try the artificial Archimedian minnow. I had never even seen this bait, but felt a great contempt for it, as I had been assured by old practised fishermen that it was entirely useless, However we resolved to give it a trial, and it was soon towing astern of the boat. I was looking over the side into the deep greenish water when my rod was violently shaken and it was evident that a good fish was fast upon it. I played him for a few minutes and then lifted him into the boat, and I saw that Charles Duncan had not exaggerated the excellence of the Tingwall trout. We did not get any large ones, the biggest was perhaps a trifle above a pound in weight, but there were no small ones among them.

Having reached the end of the loch we landed and I entered a cottage there and procured a drink of fresh bland, of which, however, Caley declined to partake. It was now twelve o'clock and we should have to leave the loch at two, as it would take us an hour and a half at least to get back to Lerwick. A light breeze now fanned the waters of the Loch, and leaving Caley to pursue the trial with the Archimedian minnow I went ashore on the eastern side, and tying on a Greenmantle with a Dun Professor as the tail fly, I commenced fishing from the shore. About one o'clock I found the trout beginning to rise well, particularly in the narrow part of the loch opposite to the holm near its southern end. Here I captured some fine trout, one of which Caley, when we got on board the steamboat this evening, amused himself by sketching. I have never, I think, seen handsomer trout than these, and Mr C. Duncan has often taken three or four dozen of this average size in an evening. It was plain that the sport was now only beginning, and it was equally clear that it must immediately terminate for two o'clock had come, and with a heavy heart I put up my rod, helped Caley to draw up the minister's boat, and then we turned our backs on Tingwall Loch, in all probability never to return to its banks.

I did not see the excellent old minister, Dr Turnbull, he rarely now received strangers after the terrible calamity that overwhelmed his family some years ago. In a severe winter about the year 1840 the loch was completely frozen over, a rare occurrence in Shetland. The wife of Mr Turnbull with her two children and a servant girl had gone out to walk on the level ice. When nearly opposite to the manse and at no great distance from the shore, the treacherous covering suddenly gave way and the mother and her two children were drowned. Another servant girl who had witnessed the catastrophe from the manse, and rushed to their assistance, shared the same fate, while the first servant by some means or other escaped.

At half past three, after a sharp walk, we arrived at Lerwick and stopped at a shop to purchase some of the Fair Isle knitted work of quaint and curious device. We reached our lodgings, dined hastily, packed up our luggage, discharged our most moderate bill, and then took a boat across the Sound to apologise to Mr Hamilton and his lady for having been unable to dine with them as had yesterday been agreed upon. It was now near 5 o'clock and the steamer was to sail at six. Our boatmen pulled well and we were soon at the manse, and proceeding to the garden I secured a rubbing of the much prized Ogham stone. We then ran to the house, bid adieu to Mrs Hamilton and hastened back to the steamer which was on the point of starting. In a few minutes the bell rang and we parted from our friends, and true to her time the vessel glided quickly out of the harbour at a quarter past six. At our evening meal we had our Tingwall trout dressed for ourselves and for the captain, and the hearty old fellow pronounced them to be excellent.

NOTES:

1 Friday 9th was spent north west of Hillswick obtaining with great difficulty a specimen of the white-bellied variety of Richardson's Skua.

2 Stone axes, from the norse word 'Tordenkiler'. Charlton had asked Andrew to enquire for examples among the cottages of Uriefirth .

3 Charlton should have been qualified to judge engineering, since his brother Francis, who shared a house with him, was County Engineer for Northumberland.

10 Charlton had been in Italy at that time in 1838

Index

Note to reader: *n denotes that index item is referred to in the footnote on that page.*